DEVELOPMENTAL MOTOR ACTIVITIES FOR ALL CHILDREN—

from Theory to Practice

DEVELOPMENTAL MOTOR ACTIVITIES FOR ALL CHILDREN—

from Theory to Practice

HAROLD A. LERCH, Ph.D.
University of Florida
Gainesville, Florida

CHRISTINE B. STOPKA, Ph.D.
University of Florida
Gainesville, Florida

Library of Congress Cataloging in Publication Data:

LERCH, HAROLD A., 1938–

STOPKA, CHRISTINE, 1953–

DEVELOPMENTAL MOTOR ACTIVITIES FOR ALL CHILDREN
FROM THEORY TO PRACTICE

Cover Design: Gary Schmitt

Copy Editor: Vickie West

Library of Congress Catalog Card Number: 91-73706

ISBN: 0-697-14479-8

Printed in the United States of America by Brown & Benchmark, 2460 Kerper Boulevard, Dubuque, IA 52001.

10 9 8 7 6 5 4 3 2 1

Dedication

This book is dedicated to *all* children, regardless of ability, whose joy of learning is the inspiration for this book. May we teach them well.

Acknowledgments

The authors wish to express their heartfelt appreciation to their spouses, children, and parents whose understanding, patience, and love made it all possible.

Contents

Preface

Developmental Motor Activities for All Children is an updated, extensively revised version of a successful earlier work by authors H. Lerch, J. Becker, B. Ward, and J. Nelson entitled *Perceptual-Motor Learning*. First published in 1974 by Peek Publications, Palo Alto, California, the latter enjoyed four printings over a span of more than 15 years with circulation at the national and international levels of education.

This retitled, newly revised edition is written for teachers who are, and college students who will be, teaching children. The physical (motor), cognitive, social, and emotional needs of *all* children, regardless of ability or disability, must be addressed and met. Any doubts whatsoever on this score are eliminated by provisions of law:

—Public Law 94-142 (1975). "The Education for All the Handicapped Children Act" (renamed in 1990 as the "Individuals with Disabilities Act" or IDEA)

—Public Law 99-457 (1988). "The Infants and Toddlers Act" (designed to meet the specific physical, cognitive, language, speech, and psycho-social needs of very young children, birth to 2 years of age)

—Public Law 101-336 (1990). "American Disabilities Act" (guarantees the civil rights of all people, including their education, employment, public accommodations, transportation, state and local government operations, and access to telecommunication relay services)

Furthermore, school systems in many states are beginning to undertake a rather different educational and administrative approach from what was often seen in 1970s and 1980s. Specifically, instead of sending disabled children to one or two "center" schools in the district, administrators have begun to "decentralize" instruction. Translation: the teaching of children with varying, severe, and even multiple exceptionalities is now *everyone's* business. Center schools for the disabled are being abandoned, and exceptional children are being integrated into "regular" schools. As there will no longer be these center schools, this new approach, coupled with the pervasive budget reductions facing most districts, means that the full-time adapted physical education specialist (who generally worked at the county's one center school, or traveled itinerantly between two to four center schools) will be increasingly harder to find. Therefore, the classroom teacher, the physical education teacher, and the special education teacher will be charged more and more with the responsibility of providing all children, regardless of exceptionality with the appropriate motor developmental activity programs for their age, interests, abilities, and needs.

In order to facilitate the effective teaching of motor activities, this book will (1) examine motor theories, of both past and present, (2) present guidelines for implementing appropriate assessment and curriculum instruments in the motor domain for these children, (3) offer a myriad of motor activity examples, including suggestions for appropriate mainstreaming via structure, methodologic intervention, and the use of adapted equipment. In addition, the reader should find the appendixes helpful; they present further administrative information, educational materials, and more to help the educator confidently embrace the challenge of providing effective and enjoyable motor activities for all of our children.

Part I   Developing an Understanding of the Need for Motor Activities

1

Moving Toward Discovery

You are never given a wish without also being given the power to make it true . . .

You may have to work for it, however.

Richard Bach

Johnny has a problem. Outwardly he looks like any other normal, healthy six-year-old boy. His eyes are bright and expressive, and he seems eager to learn. Yet beneath his carefree exterior there is a deeply troubled little boy. For Johnny is not keeping pace with his classmates when it comes to learning in the classroom. Johnny's parents, both college educated and above average in intelligence, are at a loss to understand why their son is having this difficulty. Johnny's first grade teacher agrees with his parents and adds, "Johnny appears to be bright and intelligent, but there seems to be some obstacle that he cannot overcome." By all the standards normally used to determine the learning ability of children, this youngster should be an average achiever. For example, he scores well within the average range on IQ tests. Yet when it comes to his performance in the classroom, he consistently ranks below average.

Is Johnny an isolated case? Do other children suffer from similar "mysterious" learning problems? Well, let us look at some of Johnny's classmates and see. Mary hates to read; as each day goes by she becomes more frustrated because she cannot read. Billy claims his stomach hurts when it is time for the class arithmetic lesson. Mike appears to know how to write and he has a lot of good ideas, but they are very hard for someone else to understand because Mike writes some of the letters of the alphabet backwards.

$$\top \alpha \circlearrowleft \quad \text{(cat)}$$

$$\alpha \cap b \quad \text{(and)}$$

Obviously, Johnny is not an isolated case at all. In fact, educational experts have estimated that as many as 4 out of every 10 elementary school children in the United States may have unexplained learning problems. The majority of these children are like Johnny and his friends in that their learning problems are not readily explainable. One can, therefore, begin to realize the crucial importance of understanding how children learn and of discovering how breakdowns in the learning process occur. Only through such an understanding is it possible to really help children with learning problems.

Let us take a closer look at Johnny. In the course of a normal school day he seems to be less active than most of his friends, especially on the playground. He usually stands out because he does not join in. When his friends are happily playing games, Johnny can usually be found standing on the sidelines just watching. But even when he does occasionally join in, his movements are awkward and clumsy. For some reason the ball eludes Johnny when he tries to kick it, yet it finds the tip of his nose quite well when he tries to catch it.

Is there a connection between Johnny's learning problems in the classroom and his poor motor performance on the playground? It seems as though his friends who are also having problems in the classroom also have movement problems while at play. Mary, our frustrated reader, continually loses her balance while trying to walk across a balance beam. Billy, who becomes upset just thinking about arithmetic, has unusual difficulty in attempting to tie his shoelaces. Mike, our backwards writer, does not know his right from his left. Furthermore, he cannot identify some of his body parts, nor can he coordinate their movements.

Cases such as these have caused people concerned with children's learning problems to attempt to discover if there is a relationship between how children move and how they learn. The results of numerous scientific and empirical observations have convinced a growing number of these people that such a relationship does exist. This concept is termed *perceptual-motor theory* because it appears that how individuals move and how they perceive their surroundings are all somehow interrelated and interdependent with their ability to learn.

But how? Well, first of all it is important to determine what is known about learning.[1] Actually, we do not really know a great deal about how children learn. Learning is called a "theoretical construct" because it is a process that cannot be seen and therefore must be inferred. Hence, the term perceptual-motor theory. Because it is not possible to look into the brain and see "learning" taking place, one can only make intelligent guesses as to how this process occurs. We do know, however, that in order for learning to take place there needs to be some type of sensory information transmitted to the brain.[2] Once this information reaches the brain it is interpreted and given meaning in light of previous information; we call this perception. Therefore, learning is dependent upon perceptions. If these perceptions are based upon previous motor experiences then we can see how learning is indeed motor based. (See figure 1-1.)

Assume that Johnny and his friends do have learning problems that are motor based. How then did they come to have these motor problems? Experts in the area of child growth and development such as Jean Piaget tell us that children develop in stages. The earliest and most important stage is motor development. Infants in the first few weeks of life, even before their eyes can focus properly, learn about their surroundings primarily through movement. A baby learns what a rattle is, for in-

---

[1] *Learning* will herein be defined as those permanent changes in behavior brought about by experiences.

[2] It is necessary to make a distinction between sensation and perception. These two terms will be used throughout this book. Although these terms are very closely related, they are not synonymous. *Sensation* refers to information coming into the organism through the sensory organs. *Perception*, on the other hand, although initiated by sensation, involves interpretive or cognitive processes such as discriminating, recognizing, or identifying the stimulus being sensed. Therefore, perception is greatly influenced by learning.

DEVELOPMENTAL MOTOR ACTIVITIES

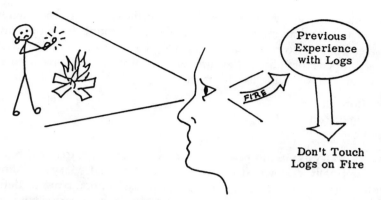

Figure 1-1. *Sensory information comes into the brain and interacts with past information leading to behavior modification.*

stance, by shaking it, by exploring it with both hands and mouth, and by bringing it close. These first crude motor explorations of the child's environment form the foundation of all future learnings.

You may ask a what a newborn baby has to do with a school-age child. The school-age child, having a fairly well-developed perceptual system, learns more about the environment through vision and hearing than through motor movements. However, upon what type of information are these perceptions based? Let us take a piece of sandpaper for an example. When you look at sandpaper you know that it has a rough surface. Our first inclination would be to say that we made that judgement by visual perception. But is this really true? Have your eyeballs ever rubbed up against sandpaper. We hope not! How then were you able to determine that sandpaper has a rough surface just by looking at it? Actually, at some time you had probably run your fingers across some sandpaper. After doing this a couple of times, you were able to translate this motor experience into a learned response, so that by simply seeing sandpaper you could decide that it is indeed a rough surface. This is called a *perceptual-motor match*. Now you can see how a learning experience that we would tend to label as a perceptual process is in reality a motor-perceptual learning process. Therefore, perceptual-motor- theorists claim that if learning is dependent upon perceptions and perceptions are dependent upon previous motor experiences, then learning is ultimately dependent upon motor activities.

One of the primary areas of investigation concerning the role of the motor system in learning has been in reading. Considering that many of the children with learning problems have trouble learning to read and that reading forms the cornerstone of our entire educational system, we can appreciate why so much research has been concentrated in this area. Another reason for studying reading has been the already discussed close connection between vision and previous motor experiences.

To help us further understand the relationship between the child's motor system and learning to read, let us take a closer look at Mary. Mary, like Johnny, is a child of "average" intelligence. Yet when she tries to read her progress is slow and painful. Mary's concerned parents took her to a vision specialist in hope of finding a solution to her problem. Upon careful examination, it was discovered that the muscles that control the movement of the eyes were not functioning properly. Therefore, Mary did not have complete control over her eye movements. Obviously, it was very hard for her to follow the words in her book in an orderly way. In fact, when she was asked to read aloud, what emerged was a jumble of disconnected words and phrases. Her eyes were unable to move smoothly from left to right, and, to make matters worse, they jumped from line to line and skipped entire words as well. When asked to read line two in the following list, Mary read, "Run, Bob, go":

1. See <u>Bob</u> run.
2. <u>Run</u> Spot run.
3. Spot can <u>go</u>.

As we can see, Mary's eyes jumped from line two, to line one, to line three. When her difficulty was finally discovered, it became apparent that Mary's reading problem really stemmed from a visual perceptual problem based upon a motor deficiency.

Could it be that Johnny and his friends were somehow deprived of essential motor experiences during the crucial early period of their development? Could there have been some type of breakdown in the developmental sequences of each of these children? If so, what could cause such a breakdown? Actually, there are a number of different potential causes. One of the more obvious is some kind of neurological injury. Brain-damaged children often exhibit significant learning problems.

Another cause of developmental breakdown is cultural deprivation. It is easy to see the difference between children who have been raised in culturally enriched homes and those not as fortunate. Culturally deprived, or "at-risk," children have not had nearly as many opportunities to touch and explore many varied objects. Consequently, the variety of experiences is less than what it could be. Only recently has this factor been appreciated, however—we tend to assume that all children entering our schools have had the same background of experiences upon which to draw.

Two other causes of breakdowns in the developmental sequence of children are emotional stresses and physical impairments. In many instances, these factors are easily recognizable, but not always. Emotional trauma, for example, can have a devastating effect on development. Take the child who experiences a bad fall at his first attempt to walk. Who can tell what effect this experience and the resultant hesitation to try again will have on the child's future development?

At this point a number of important questions need to be answered. First, does the fact that the perceptual-motor concept is essentially theoretical and controversial mean that educational practitioners should take a "wait and see" attitude and not attempt to apply these theories to their children until more research "proof" is available? It is our belief that research needs to be done at both the laboratory and action levels. This means that informed practitioners in the field can lend a great deal to our knowledge in this area through action research with their children. Secondly, what is the target population of perceptual-motor concept programs in the schools? The perceptual-motor concept would have its greatest application with children of "average" intelligence who are underachieving. The earlier these children can be spotted the better, so preschool programs such as Project Head Start would not be too early. Elementary school kindergarten through grade three offers the greatest opportunity to spot problems in the perceptual-motor area. After the third grade, indications are that learning problems become more specific. Remedial perceptual-motor programs can be initiated by classroom teachers or physical education specialists.

Finally, how can perceptual-motor theory be applied to the school setting? It can be applied in two ways: (1) through screening tests, and then (2) through developmental motor activities. For example, the classroom teacher or the physical education specialist can easily administer a screening test which measures both the large muscle and fine motor abilities of children who are experiencing learning difficulties. Part II of this book includes an example of a basic large muscle and fine motor screening test. In addition, we present many other motor tests and analyze them as to purpose, content to be assessed, population type, and important administrative considerations.

Once the children with motor, behavioral, or cognitive deficiencies have been identified, the next step is to organize the educational team needed to address these deficiencies. This team is called the child's individual educational program (or plan) team, often referred to as the IEP team. The IEP team is normally made up of the classroom teacher, a physical education specialist, a reading specialist, the parents, a vision specialist, and the school psychologist. The needs of the situation may dictate other team members such as physical therapists.

After the IEP team has been organized, each member will have a specific portion of the remedial program to administer. In the case of the physical education specialist and the classroom teacher, it is imperative that the child continue to attend the regular physical education program rather than be removed from this valuable motor activity time for other remedial activities. In conjunction with the physical education program, and based upon specific areas of weakness, the child's IEP should include a program of developmental motor activities. For example, if this child has shown a marked weakness in balance skills, the IEP should include an individualized, systematic, progressive program of balance activities geared toward any specific weaknesses and planned to emphasize success and enjoyment.

Developmental motor activities can be planned and implemented to address virtually any motor area in need of reinforcement or remediation. Part III of this book is devoted to specific developmental activities to match the areas tested on the screening test. In each case, if a child shows weakness in a particular area, we present a number of activities and suggestions for working with the child.

2

Developmental Learning Theories

To learn to think, therefore, we should exercise our limbs, and our organs, which are the instruments of our intelligence.

Rousseau, Emile

How do children learn? We are only beginning to answer this question. In the first chapter, we met Johnny and some fellow students with learning problems and determined that *possibly* there was a connection between their classroom difficulties and their various motor problems. But what kind of connection? Certainly something more or less tangible like a visual deficiency, a short attention span, or a behavioral problem could be the cause of Johnny's difficulties in both the motor and the academic areas. However, the premise that an isolated motor weakness may be the reason for a particular academic skill deficiency is unfounded. The "classic" perceptual-motor theory of learning, that improved motor performance will directly improve cognitive performance, was once a subject of speculation and debate, but is currently unsupported by research. Also, although it seems only logical that an improved self-concept due to a successful accomplishment in one area (such as a motor skill) may generalize to helping the child feel better about learning in other areas (such as some academic skills), solid proof for even such *indirect* effects remains elusive.

What we can be sure of is specificity: A specific weakness in a certain area demands specific attention (i.e., teaching and practice) in that area. If the teaching is well planned and implemented, improvement in that specific area of weakness can be expected. How much this new learning will spill over to other areas of weakness is simply unknown at this time.

To summarize, we currently believe that motor problems can be ameliorated by appropriate motor programming, but it remains to be demonstrated that a child's improved motor performance also helps the child's cognitive performance. Before deciding if this is the final word, we need to appreciate how we have arrived at this conclusion. A brief historical summary of our thinking on this topic shall illustrate where we have been, where we are now, and where we may go with future research on this topic.

A BRIEF HISTORICAL PERSPECTIVE

In the past, individuals from such different fields as psychology, optometry, and education, supported the perceptual-motor theory. In this section, we will examine the writings of some of history's foremost perceptual-motor theorists in an attempt to understand why they asserted so strongly that "all learning begins with movement."

Piaget

In trying to understand the process by which learning takes place, one logical starting point is to study children as they grow up. Through such a study, one can try to find out how the helpless newborn goes about mastering the complex process of exploring and taking in information about the environment, and eventually develops the ability to deal with that environment symbolically (i.e., through the use of letters and numbers which make up our language). This ability, known as *cognition*, separates humans from the lower animals. One of the earliest investigators from the developmental point of view to study how children learn and to come to the conclusion that all higher learnings are based on early motor experiences was the Swiss psychologist, Jean Piaget (Flavel, 1963; Piaget & Inhelder, 1969).

Piaget identifies a number of developmental stages which he claims children pass through in the development of their cognitive abilities. The first period of life Piaget labels the *sensorimotor* stage. This stage covers approximately the first two years of children's lives. During these years children change from being self-centered infants who respond to the environment through primitive reflexes (such as sucking) to being children capable of rather complex sensorimotor[1] interactions with their environment. The period from age 2 to 11 is subdivided into two stages, the *preoperational* period and the period of *concrete operations*. The preoperational period (ages 2-7) is characterized by children's initial attempts to deal with their world symbolically. (See figure 2-1 and 2-2.) The period of concrete operations (ages 7-11) is the period in which children begin to organize their understanding of their environment, and to develop the ability to knowingly adapt to changing situations. And, finally, there is

Figure 2-1. *Children first experience objects then verbalize concepts related to those objects.*

---

[1]Sensorimotor here refers to the complex cycle whereby children take in information about the environment through their senses (touch, sight, hearing, smell, taste) and react to these sensations with a motor response.

DEVELOPMENTAL MOTOR ACTIVITIES

Figure 2-2. *Children learn to translate the visual image of an object into the word representation of that object.*

the period of *formal operations* (ages 11-15) in which children develop the ability not only to deal effectively with concrete situations, but to deal with purely abstract situations as well.

Of these periods, the sensorimotor stage is the most crucial; it is during this period that the foundations are laid for the higher learnings which will develop later. Therefore, we should look a bit closer at this period. (Piaget terms this the sensorimotor period because it is during this period (before speech) that children lack the ability to substitute abstractions such as words and thoughts for the concrete realities which they represent. This does not mean, however, that intelligence does not exist before language; Piaget contents that the child has a basically practical intelligence founded on sensory perceptions and movements. By "practical" he means that it is focused on getting results which benefit the child. Children, therefore, are capable of solving movement problems, such as reaching distant objects, because they relate these problems to a movement vocabulary which they are developing, of increasingly complex movement experiences.

Piaget has subdivided the sensorimotor stage into six substages. During Stage 1, or the first month of children's lives, they make use of automatic reflexes such as sucking, swallowing, crying, and the like. Children are, of course, born with these reflexes, and Piaget emphasizes that during this stage they begin to modify their reflexive behavior in response to the environment. That is, children soon begin to suck in response to stimulation around the area of the mouth. This represents the first stage of development: the child, not the reflex, starts the response.

Stage 2, or the period from 1 to 4 months, is highlighted by children developing the ability to coordinate the use of more than one sense at a time. They can, for example, reach out and touch an object brought into their field of vision, combining both visual and tactile (touch) sensations in a coordinated manner. It is also during this period that the first simple habits are formed.

Stage 3, approximately from 4 to 5 months, is characterized by children handling everything that comes near them. Children now have the ability to cause something to happen; in other words, they begin to assert control over their environment.

In Stages 4 and 5, the period from 8 to 18 months, children begin to understand the difference between means and ends. They will, for example, attempt different methods to obtain an object out of their reach. Children then will get to the point of searching for new means to reach a desired end, such as pulling a rug toward themselves to obtain an object which they could not otherwise reach.

Finally, in Stage 6, which runs from 18 months to 2 years, children begin to bridge the gap from this sensorimotor stage to the following periods. They do this by inventing means to achieve desired ends, such as utilizing a stick to reach an object that is out of reach.

Now consider Piaget's explanation of the development of perception. He is firmly convinced of the role of movement in the development of intelligence and states, "as regards the development of the cognitive functions in the child . . . the sensorimotor structures constitute the source of the later operations of thought. This means that intelligence proceeds from action as a whole" (Piaget & Inhelder, 1969, p. 28).

Piaget discounts the idea that mental life stems only from sensation and reason and does not involve action. To completely understand the error of this line of reasoning, he feels we must examine the role of the sensorimotor system in the development of perceptions. He points out that it is extremely difficult to follow the development of perception in the young infant because the baby cannot be subjected to precise laboratory experiments. There are however, two visual perceptual abilities that can be studied in relation to sensorimotor functions during the first year. The first is *constancy* which may be subdivided into constancy of form and constancy of size.

Constancy of form refers to the perception of an object as it would appear from a frontal view, regardless of its present position. *Constancy of size* refers to the perception of the real size of an object when viewed from a distance, even though it appears to be shrinking. These constancies appear in the child about the middle of the first year. (See figure 2-3 and 2-4.)

Figure 2-3. *Children with properly developed constancy of form see the bottle from the bottom but perceive it in their minds in its upright position.*

Figure 2-4. *Children with properly developed constancy of size see an object at a distance, yet perceive it in their mind in its real size.*

DEVELOPMENTAL MOTOR ACTIVITIES

Piaget bases his belief that constancy of form is dependent upon motor activity on his observations of the relationship between constancy of form and the permanence of an object. Children gradually come to understand that when an object disappears, it does not cease to exist. He explains that very young children discover that objects are permanent through motor activities related to those objects. Piaget uses the example of babies who are given a bottle with the bottom turned toward them but who fail to recognize it as a bottle. Obviously, these children do not perceive a constant form of the bottle. However, later on children will know to readily turn the bottle around as they have learned to search for hidden objects (i.e., when they have established the permanence of objects), thus indicating that object permanence and constancy of form are related. Because of this, Piaget assumes that an interaction takes place between perception and motor activity.

Piaget then points out that constancy of size appears after children have developed the ability to coordinate their vision with the handling of objects. This helps explain why constancy of size cannot exist before this time. If visual and tactile sensations are not coordinated, the size of an object would remain constant to the touch but variable to the sight. Therefore, it is the sensorimotor development of the child that forms the basis for visual-tactile coordination essential to constancy of size perception. (See figure 2-5.)

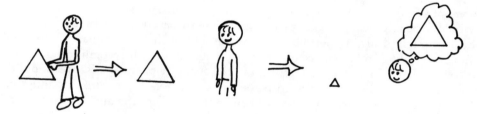

Figure 2-5. *Children must coordinate what they see with what they feel before perceiving constancy of size.*

The second visual perceptual ability which can be determined in very young children is perceptual causality. If a child observes one object strike another, and because of the impact the second object moves, the child has the impression that the first object caused the second to move. Depending on how the two striking objects react after impact, the observer has impressions of resistance, weight, and thrust. None of these impressions, of course, are visual in origin. This is, therefore, a case of tactile and kinesthetic impressions which have been translated into corresponding visual terms. (See figure 2-6.)

Figure 2-6. *Perceptual impressions of resistance, weight, and thrust are based on movement experiences with objects. Therefore, visual impressions of these phenomena depend on prior motor experiences.*

DEVELOPMENTAL LEARNING THEORIES

Piaget summarizes his beliefs on the development of perception by saying:

Generally speaking, then, we see that perceptual activities develop with age until they are able to obey the directives of the intelligence. But before the operations of thought are formed, it is the global action (motor activities) which performs the role of orientation. (Piaget & Inhelder, 1969, p. 43)

Hebb

Another early theorist to support the notion that intellectual development is at least partially dependent upon motor development was D.O. Hebb.

In his book, *The Organization of Behavior* (1949) Hebb set about to clarify what he considered to be a misconception concerning the role of motor activity in perception. Psychologists had long before discarded the idea that perception was based solely on motor activity. This theory had been replaced, however, by what Hebb felt to be just as false a theory that perception occurred completely independent of motor activity. After much investigation and careful consideration, Hebb decided that neither extreme position was correct, but rather that although motor activity was an important factor in perception, it was not all-important.

To illustrate his position Hebb used the example of the relationship of eye movement (a motor activity) to visual perception. Ordinary visual perception, which we would probably assume takes place somewhat automatically, actually is the end product of a long learning period in humans and other higher animals. Perceptual learning, according to Hebb, occurs gradually beginning with recognition of dominant colors, then proceeding to attention to the separate parts of a figure, and ultimately culminating in the ability to recognize the whole figure. Infants must go through this complex learning sequence before they acquire the ability to recognize an object at a single glance.

In recognizing the form of a square, for example, the infant must first learn to identify the various parts of the figure over a period of time. Hebb feels that this identification depends upon visual scanning of the figure, requiring a number of eye movements. The figure does not, at this stage of perceptual development, appear simply as a whole, but rather it appears to be several parts which are distinct from the whole. Once this first learning stage is mastered, Hebb points out that eye movements are no longer essential; but even for mature adults, eye movements definitely add to the clarity of perception. (See figure 2-7.) Therefore, if we return to our example of the perception of a square, we can see that we did not always immediately recognize this figure as a square, but rather that this recognition is the result of a long, slow learning process which originally depended on many eye movements.

Closely associated with the above illustration is that of the relationship of eye movements to the formation of a visual image on the brain. Hebb contends that it would be difficult if not impossible to have an image of a given figure without making a number of eye movements. For example, in viewing a figure such as a triangle, circle, or square, children would make several eye movements possibly jumping from point to point; but they would not simply fix the object in space. These eye movements, according to Hebb, not only improve the image but are essential to the development of vision.

Figure 2-7. *Initially, young children scan an object with their eyes and recognize its various parts. Once they have learned this, children can recognize the object at a single glance.*

The final step in this chain of logic is to answer the question concerning what role the motor area (cortex) of the brain plays in visual perception. Obviously, the motor cortex would not be involved at all unless perception was in some way closely related to motor activity. As there is no evidence to support the possibility that the motor cortex of the brain actually receives visual sensation, it would, therefore, follow that it must somehow be involved with the changing of incoming sensations into visual perceptions. Hebb (1949) concludes his discussion of the importance of motor activity in visual perception by saying that

> Receptor adjustment (head-and-eye movement) is the most prominent feature of visual perception . . . except in long-practiced habits . . . eye movements in perception . . . contribute, constantly and essentially, to perceptual integration, even though they are not the whole origin of it. (p. 37)

Delacato

In 1959, a book was published that was destined to have a profound influence on the thinking of those individuals involved with children with learning problems—particularly those children with reading problems. This book, *The Treatment and Prevention of Reading Problems* (1959) by Carl H. Delacato, represented a departure from the traditional practice of seeking to correct reading problems by changing the system or method of teaching reading. Delacato points out that this latter approach has been tried time and again. Although methods have varied, and new methods have been invented to teach children to read (such as sight recognition, phonetic, etc.), invariably whatever method was used some children would learn how to read and some would not. He, therefore, reasoned that some children would learn to read under any method, whereas certain other children would not learn under any method. This led him to look for the cause of reading problems not in the methods of teaching reading but rather within the children themselves.

Is there some factor or set of factors inherent within children that makes it either difficult or impossible for them to learn to read? If so, what are these factors and how may they be corrected? Delacato began a research project to attempt to answer these questions and others. He chose as subjects 45 boys[2] ranging in age from 8 to 10 who were experiencing reading problems. The results of this study indicated that there are a number of traits that seem to characterize the poor reader. All of these common traits were either physical or developmental. Delacato analyzed his results and decided that the primary area of concern was the neurological area. In other words, the problems which children with reading difficulties experience are in some way related to problems within their own central nervous system.

In effect, Delacato's investigations revived the old theory that the neurological development of an individual follows the evolutionary development of the nervous system in humans. That is, the nervous system in humans represents the ultimate neurological development achieved in the animal kingdom. As the human nervous system evolved throughout the centuries, it developed from a very simple to a very complex system. Most of the human central nervous system, such as the spinal cord, mid-brain, and other areas, resembles that of other animals. The primary difference between man and the lower animals is in the development of the cerebral cortex. (See figure 2-8.)

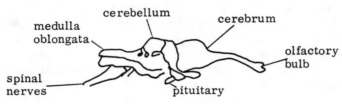

Typical animal brain (Alligator)

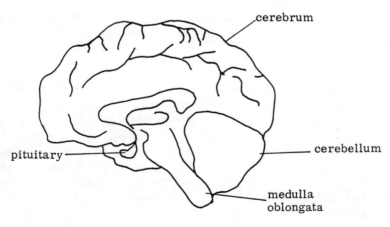

Figure 2-8. *Typical human brain.*

It is this highly developed cerebral cortex that gives humans the power of thought and reason which separates us from lower animals. The cerebral cortex, according to Delacato, allows humans to develop cortical dominance through which

---

[2]He chose boys rather than girls because available research indicated that 4 boys have reading problems for every 1 girl experiencing the same problem.

one side of the body becomes dominant over the other. The cortex of the brain is divided into two parts or hemispheres. The right side of the brain controls the left side of the body and vice versa. If the left side of the brain were dominant, for example, then the right side of the body would be also. This is a highly desirable condition; when it is absent, the individual has not gone through the proper neurological developmental pattern. This individual is, therefore, said to have neurological disorganization, which results in reading and communication failures. (See figure 2-9.)

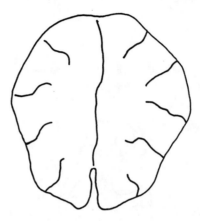

Figure 2-9. *Human brain (top view). The human brain is divided into two hemispheres. According to Delacato, if the left hemisphere is dominant, then the right side of the body should be dominant because the left side of the brain controls the right side of the body.*

The importance of cerebral dominance lies at the heart of Delacato's theories concerning the treatment and prevention of reading problems in children. He points out that until about age 6½, most children are ambidextrous (can use either hand equally well); at this time they usually develop a dominant eye, hand, and foot. Because reading is taught at age 6½, and this is the age when dominance is formed, then handedness and reading are controlled by the dominant hemisphere. On the other hand, from birth the subdominant area of the brain controls the nondominant functions such as tonality (the quality of tones as in music or the voice). Children exhibit tonal qualities at birth by (making various sounds), and most children initially tend to be left-handed, even though as they grow up most will become right-handed. Children, therefore, develop in the subdominant area first. As they learn to talk, and dominance appears on one side, we can then assume that the dominant hemisphere is in control.

Stuttering also, Delacato claims, is the result of lack of cerebral dominance. As most stutterers do not stutter while singing, he attributes this to the subdominant area, which controls tonality, actually being in control.

Delacato also observed both good and poor readers during sleep and noticed a definite difference in the sleep pattern of both groups. When good readers sleep in a prone position (on their stomachs), their arms and legs are flexed on the side of the body that the head is facing, while the arms and legs on the opposite side are extended. (See figure 2-10.) When the head is turned in the opposite direction, a sequence

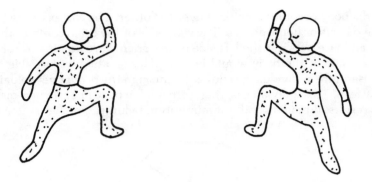

Figure 2-10. *Delacato found that good readers sleep with their arm and leg flexed on the side of the body the head faces, even when the head changes from one side to the other.*

Figure 2-11. *With* poor *readers, Delacato found this pattern did not occur.*

of events occurs in which the arm and leg on the side of the body the head is facing flex, and the arm and leg on the opposite side extend.

Poor readers, it was found, do not sleep in this position, and if their heads are placed in this position the sequential reflex does not take place. (See figure 2-11.) This indicates a lack of neurological organization which prevents the sequential reflex action from taking place. This, Delacato explains, is why so many poor readers are classified as uncoordinated in movement activities such as running and walking. They simply do not have the neurological organization necessary to coordinate the movements in an efficient, meaningful pattern. Thus, without developing sequential patterns of movement, poor readers are uncoordinated at both the gross (large muscle) and fine (small muscle) motor levels.

Delacato also explains how slight brain damage in children may possibly cause reading disabilities. Obviously, those children with severe brain damage can be easily identified and would be expected to experience reading problems. But what about those children with very slight brain damage which is not easy to spot? For example, we know that anoxia (a lack of oxygen) for a period of three minutes can have a devastating effect on human brain cells. An infant deprived of oxygen for this period of time, either at birth or prior to birth, would surely be mentally handicapped because of the large number of brain cells destroyed. Delacato, therefore, reasoned that if a

DEVELOPMENTAL MOTOR ACTIVITIES

three-minute oxygen loss caused severe brain damage, a one-minute oxygen loss might also cause minor brain damage. This damage might not be great enough to be seen in obvious movement and mental handicaps, but may be enough to affect those highly sensitive brain cells responsible for the development of language.

The potential damage resulting from oxygen loss might answer the question of why four times as many boys experience reading problems as do girls. Delacato explains this by citing evidence that boys' heads tend to be larger at birth, thus lengthening the birth process and significantly increasing the period of time between dependence on the mother for oxygen and breathing for themselves. This would also help to explain why more firstborn children, as well as boys, tend to experience reading problems, because deliveries of firstborn children are also slower.

Delacato investigated the role of vision in reading and came to some very interesting conclusions. He feels that visual dominance is just as important as hand and foot dominance in determining the ability of a child to read. Accordingly, hand, food, and eye dominance should all appear on the same side of the child's body if proper neurological organization is present. If the above conditions exist, the child should be able to read well.

Delacato points out that three qualities of vision should be evaluated to determine if proper neurological organization exists in the child. First, the dominant or the sighting eye should be determined. This is usually the eye used to look through a telescope (or a rolled up piece of paper). This eye serves a monocular (one-eyed) function, is established early in life, and stays the same throughout life. Secondly, the controlling eye should be determined. During binocular vision both eyes are used at the same time, but one eye actually controls the perception while the other serves in an assisting roll. To determine the controlling eye, one holds the index finger out at arms length in front of the face. Now one should pick out a distant object and, with both eyes open, "cover" the object with the index finger. Now one should close the left eye. If the object is still covered then the right eye is the controlling eye. If, however, the finger has "moved," the left eye is the controlling eye. This can be checked again by now closing the right eye and opening the left. This "controlling eye" is not necessarily also the dominant eye. Contrary to the stability of the dominant eye, the controlling eye may be shifted due to changes in vision or actually be changed through training.

Finally, the reading-visual function of each eye should be determined to find out which eye is more efficient. Testing by occlusion (covering of one eye) to see which eye reads material faster and with the fewest mistakes easily demonstrates the difference in efficiency of the two eyes. In each of the above mentioned cases, the dominant eye, the controlling eye, and the most efficient eye should be on the dominant side (i.e., the same side as the preferred hand and foot). If all three do not fall on the same side, crossed dominance and neurological disorganization is indicated and remedial measures (such as occlusion of the subdominant eye) are called for.

In his second book, *The Diagnosis and Treatment of Speech and Reading Problems* (1963), Delacato carefully traces the neurological development of the child. He describes the corresponding motor activity of each stage of development. He then compares the child's neurological development with animals that represent various levels of neurological development on the evolutionary scale. (See figure 2-12.) For example, the behavior of newborn children is primarily reflexive in nature; that is, their actions are controlled by life-supporting reflexes such as breathing.

DEVELOPMENTAL LEARNING THEORIES

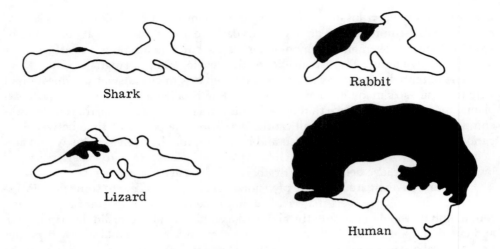

Figure 2-12. *Various brains representing stages of neurological development within the animal kingdom. Dark areas indicate the relative proportion of brain area devoted to thinking.*

These reflexes are under the control of the most primitive area of the human brain, the medulla oblongata. The child's motor actions at this time are fish-like in character, and, indeed, the fish represents an animal which on the evolutionary scale develops no further than to this primitive neurological level.

At approximately 4 months of age, the child moves into the next neurological level. During this period the child begins to crawl. This method of locomotion is made with the body in contact with the floor. The body moves with homolateral movements of the arms and legs, with the arm and leg on one side of the body bent while the arm and leg on the opposite side are straight. This type of movement pattern, typical of amphibians in water, seems to be controlled by the pons. (See figure 2-13.)

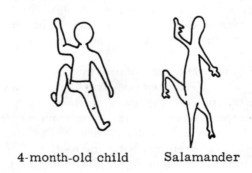

4-month-old child   Salamander

Figure 2-13.

The pons represents the next step above the medulla in the neurological organization of the brain, and this is the most important part of the amphibian brain.

At approximately 6 months the child begins to creep. Creeping involves not only moving about on the hands and knees but doing so in a cross-pattern manner. Cross-pattern creeping means that as the child's left arm moves forward, the right leg moves forward at the same time. In the next movement, the child's right arm moves forward as the left leg moves forward. As the child moves across the floor, the arm and leg movements are alternated in this manner, and the child will also turn the head slightly in the direction of the forward hand. This activity is similar to the manner in which reptiles move across the ground, and according to Delacato, it is the mid-brain which controls this action in both children and reptiles. In reptiles the main feature of the brain is the mid-brain; the child, therefore, has reached the neurological development level of the reptile—or equal to the evolutionary stage of the mid-brain. (See figure 2-14.)

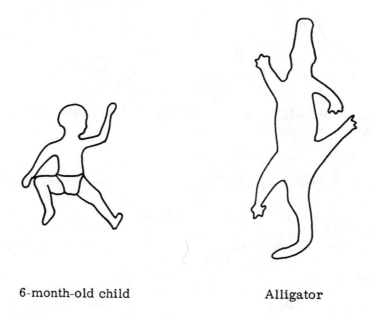

6-month-old child   Alligator

Figure 2-14.

At around 1 year children begin to pull themselves up on furniture, and they begin a crude form of walking characterized by the arms working independently of the legs. Delacato points out that if the cross-patterning of the mid-brain state is not mastered, the child will show signs of neurological disorganization and will have difficulty in mastering walking. This form of crude walking is typical of primates (mammals such as monkeys, which are considered to be the nearest evolutionary level to humans). Primates have brains in which the cortex is similar to that of humans. The cortex of primates does not, of course, develop the efficiency of the human cortex; so during this stage children, according to Delacato, most resemble primates in their displays of early cortical action. (See figure 2-15.)

Between 5 and 8 years, children develop the hemispheric dominance that separates them from the rest of the animal kingdom. During this period children should develop one side of the body as dominant. Also, they should have a cross-pattern walking style similar to that which they had developed in cross-pattern creeping (i.e., the opposite arm and leg move forward and the head turns slightly in the direction of the forward arm). Therefore, Delacato asserts, when children have mastered this fi-

1-year-old child Monkey

Figure 2-15.

nal stage at approximately 8 years, they have reached the final level of neurological development in the evolutionary scale.

Kephart

In 1960 another book was published that had as its central theme the role of the motor system in learning disabilities. This book, *The Slow Learner in the Classroom* (1960) by Newell C. Kephart, was written expressly for classroom and special teachers working with children with learning difficulties. The basis of both this book, and of *Success Through Play* (Radler & Kephart, 1960), a book interpreting Kephart's works for the layman, is the observation that many children coming to school for the first time lack the "readiness" to learn. That is, we assume that children coming to school possess certain underlying abilities such as being able to control their eye movements, which will allow them to achieve success in school. Kephart believes many children lack these important perceptual and motor abilities, therefore handicapping them in their efforts to learn. He feels, however, that these readiness skills are as much learned as they are developed through maturation, and that they can be taught in the school situation.

The complexity of the environment confronting children, according to Kephart, makes any learning task difficult and demands that their behavior in response to the environment be flexible and coordinated. In tracing the growth of young children, Kephart points out that they learn by doing. Their very early responses to the environment are motor responses; they are continually handling objects and moving their own bodies in relation to those objects so that they can understand their world motorically. Once children have established a "feel: for the environment, they begin to join together their motor experiences with sensory information coming in through their eyes, ears, nose, mouth, and skin. Primarily it is the eyes that are used as the extension of the arms to help investigate objects which cannot be reached. The key point here is that the visual information which children increasingly use now is based upon motor information they have been gathering. Children begin to match incoming visual information with motor information as they simultaneously handle and observe a given object. Over a period of time, children come to develop a perceptual-motor "match" in which both systems give them the same information. They actually learn to explore an object visually the same way they formerly explored it with their hands.

Kephart points out the importance of the great amount of experimentation involved in this process. Although to use this may seem rather aimless, it is for the most part very meaningful and should be started naturally by the child and not imposed by an adult. However, the problems which many children are experiencing in relating to an extremely complex society are oftentimes caused by the fewer demands made upon children to explore on their own. As adults have tried to make growing up easier for children by doing things for them or by substituting mechanical for manual toys, children are deprived of many opportunities to explore, experiment and touch—experiences they must have to form a stable perceptual-motor system. Many children raised in this manner lack adequate perceptual motor skills and are coming into our schools unable to cope with the demands made upon them. For these children a great many opportunities to develop perceptual-motor skills through extensive exploration must be provided early in their school lives so that they will not become "slow learners."

To help explain the complexities of the underlying readiness skills necessary for a child to begin school, Kephart uses the example of a 5-year-old child drawing a square. This seemingly simple task is actually only possible after many basic learning abilities are mastered. If we were to ask a child to sit at a desk and draw a square, one of the most basic large muscle abilities this child would need to have would be the ability to sit up. Observation of a young infant attempting to sit will easily show us the great amount of time involved in learning to do this seemingly natural task. To be able to sit up, the child must, of course, learn to balance, vary tension among muscle groups, and develop the necessary strength. The development of the large muscle skills necessary to maintain posture, therefore, underlies every child's ability to sit properly in a chair so that they can draw the square.

Next the child must be able to coordinate the movements of fingers, hand, wrist, and arm. This, again, seems to be a rather natural event, but as we know from observing children growing up, fine motor movements in the extremities develop only after mastery of central large muscle movements. That is, large movements of the arms come before movements in the wrist and hand which come before fine motor movements of the fingers. Thus, we can see that to be able to pick up a pencil and draw a square, the child must have passed through a long period of learning in which they develop first large muscle movements and finally fine muscle movements. Mastery of this process would allow enough control of the pencil to draw the square.

The child must also have enough muscular control to be able to call upon the proper muscles in the proper order to be able to accomplish the task of drawing the square. The child must have the control to call upon just the right set of muscles without setting into action other sets of muscles. The child must also be able to differentiate the movements of hand and fingers from total body movements, as well as to know one side of the body from the other.

Another task children must handle before they can copy the square is to separate the figure (square) from the ground (background). It is hard for us to imagine looking at a square or a printed page without seeing them as just that. Children, however, who have not developed proper form perception are apt to lose the square in its background and to confuse a printed word with elements in the background of the page. If the child has not developed this ability to distinguish parts of a figure from one another, then copying a figure such as a square or reading words on a printed page can be a hopeless task.

Thus in taking Kephart's example of copying a square we can easily see that what we might have considered as a very basic task is, in itself, actually a complex skill requiring much previous learning.

Kephart (1960) continually stresses the fundamental role that the motor system plays in the development of higher forms of behavior. He states that

> It is logical to assume that all behavior is basically motor, that the prerequisites of any kind of behavior are muscular and motor responses. Behavior develops out of muscular activity, and so-called higher forms of behavior are dependent upon lower forms of behavior, thus making even these higher activities dependent upon the basic structure of the muscular activity upon which they are built. (p. 35)

It is easy to see that certain behavior depends upon movement when one can observe parts of the body moving in response to a given stimulus. But what about non-observable, internal behavior, such as thinking? Are "thinking" children who sit apparently motionless in a chair actually using their motor system? According to Kephart (1960), they are. Experiments using sensitive electrodes placed on the skin (electromyography) have measured subjects' muscular responses to thought. Both general overall muscular tension and specific muscular tension within certain muscle groups increase under these circumstances. Thus, what we might describe as "pure thought" processes actually involve muscular activity. It is therefore possible, implies Kephart, that the higher thought processes are no more efficient than the muscular responses upon which they are based.

One of the most basic of all movement patterns is that of posture. The importance of proper posture in copying a square has already been discussed, but posture plays another role in learning. It is through posture that we maintain a fixed orientation with our environment. If we are to have a set reference point from which to interact with the objects around us, it must be based on the force of gravity. We must establish a relationship with gravity through our own center of gravity and be aware of this relationship in all of our activities. Only through this stable relationship with gravity can we maintain a point of reference for interaction with our environment.

Closely related to posture as a point of reference for the body is laterality. Kephart (1960) explains that outside of our own body there is no information concerning direction. We develop information concerning right and left from within our own bodies. This information comes as the result of learning based on internal sensations about right and left. Every child must experiment with both sides of the body to determine their relationship to each other. Only through experimental movements of both sides of the body and through comparing these movements and the differences between them with internal sensations (kinesthesis) can children learn to tell the difference between right and left within their own bodies. The primary use of this information comes in relation to balance. Maintaining balance is a problem that is constantly confronting children. Only with knowledge of, and proper utilization of right and left (laterality) can children continually maintain their balance.

Once children have developed laterality within their own bodies, they are ready to project this concept of right and left into the surrounding space. "Directionality" refers to the concept of left and right in space, as well as all other directions (such as up, down, forward, backward, north, south, east, west, in, out, over, under, through, etc.). Again. this transfer of a concept takes place gradually after much experimentation. For example, children will attempt to reach an object and in so doing will notice that they must make a movement, perhaps to the right. By repeating this process a number of times, children will come to transfer by the concept of right and left from within to objects in the surrounding space. At this point, of course, control of the eyes becomes a vitally important factor. Because the majority of information about our environment comes to us through our eyes, the development of directionality depends upon our visual system giving us the same directional information formerly obtained through kinesthesis.

Control of the eyes is also a very complex and exact motor task. The human eye is moved by six ocular muscles. These muscles have the task of moving the eye so that an image coming into the eye will fall on a small area at the back of the eyeball called the fovea. To accomplish this task, the eye must be moved with great precision. Because of this, learning to control the movement of the eye is quite difficult. In time, however, the child will learn to match the movement of the eyes with the movement of the hands so that both systems will give the same directionality information.

Yet another problem concerning directionality is that of being constrained to, and not being able to cross over, the midline. Using this as the point of reference, children make circular motions with their arms and legs at the same time. As the right arm moves toward the center of the body, the left arm moves toward the center of the body also. Moving the arms from outside in, therefore, involves going from left-to-right for the left arm and right-to-left for the right arm. A little later, when the child begins to cross the body's midline, we can easily see how confusion might set in, because to move the left hand left-to-right involves first an outside-in and then an inside-out pattern of movement. This new concept often causes children to hesitate and become confused as they cross the midline. Indeed, many older, slow-learning children show this same hesitancy and confusion.

As the child learns to transfer information about the environment from motor to visual understanding through kinesthetic-visual matches, the same transfer problem concerning crossing the midline can occur with the eyes that previously occurred with the hands. Thus, to avoid confusion the child must learn to locate the midline of his body with great accuracy and always to reverse the transfer of movement at the midline without disrupting the continuous movement. If this smooth transfer cannot be accomplished, the child will appear to be indecisive and will lose control when the eyes cross the body's midline.

To summarize the relationship of directionality to laterality, we can say that directionality is the transfer into the environment of the laterality developed within the child. Directionality is dependent upon laterality; until the child has established solid concepts of laterality within, the child will not have an accurate concept of right and left in space. To transfer laterality to directionality the child must make a match between visual information and kinesthetic information. To be able to do this the child must have exact eye control, and the child must always know in what direction the eyes are pointed. Thus, the establishment of laterality and then the establishment of directionality are possible only through motor activity and the observations of that motor activity.

If we accept Kephart's reasoning that children establish their own bodies as the point of reference in dealing with objects in the environment, it follows that children must have an accurate understanding of the dimensions of their bodies and of the position of their bodies in space. Through various sensations (i.e., pressure, pain, etc.) we develop a picture of ourselves in our own minds. Through this "body image" we develop an understanding of the relationship of our bodies to other objects in space. Children who have not established a proper body image will continually overestimate the amount of space necessary for them to perform certain movements. For example, such children, if asked to squeeze through a small space slightly larger than their own bodies, will repeatedly bump into the boundaries of this space. They will also show great difficulty in moving various body parts independently of one another. If they begin to move their right arm, their left arm may move as well. They may also have difficulty transferring visual cues, such as when one points at a given body part, into muscular action or movement of the body part indicated. Children should be able to identify and control their various body parts independently if they have developed a proper body image.

In conclusion, Kephart (1960) states his belief that the input system, or perceptions and sensations, cannot be separated from the output system, or motor responses. He, therefore, encourages thinking and talking about these two systems as being part of the same closed cycle and stresses that "we cannot think of perceptual activities and motor activities as two different items; we must think of the hyphenated term perceptual-motor" (p.63).

Getman

Now that we have studied the claims of perceptual-motor theorists that motor activity forms the basis for visual perception, it would seem appropriate to get the reaction of a vision specialist to this point of view. One such specialist, Optometrist G.N. Getman, has done research in this area and agrees with the findings of Kephart and others.

Getman (1971) points out that to the optometrist the eye is little more than a sensory organ which receives, reacts to, and changes light waves into electrical impulses which are sent to the brain. Somehow, these electrical impulses are combined in the brain with information coming in from other sensory systems. Whereas optometrists need to know about the structure and operation of the eye, they have come to realize that to fully understand how the eye functions as part of a total visual system they must study more than just the eyes. For example, it is quite possible for two individuals to have eyes that, when measured clinically, appear to be exactly the same but are functionally quite different. That is, one of the individuals may need glasses constantly while the other may need glasses only for certain tasks, even through their prescriptions are exactly the same.

At this point, it is essential that we understand the difference between sight and vision. Although we often use the two terms interchangeably, they are not synonymous. Getman (1971) defines sight and vision as follows:

Sight is the response of the eye to light, and its translation of this light into neural signals. Vision is the response of the total organism—the entire human being—to the information being collected throughout the total organism as a result of the light impact. Sight is the reception of light. Vision is the translation, utilization, and integration of the information, followed by the action of the totality in its use of this information. Whereas sight refers to the reaction of the eyes to light, vision refers to the entire complex of responses in all of the information systems as a result of the light impact. These primarily include the information systems of kinesthesis, touch, hearing, and several others. Sight can be isolated in the eyeball; vision cannot and must interchange with other systems. (p. 25)

Vision is, therefore, highly dependent upon the motor development of the individual. Because of this relationship between motor development and vision, Getman feels that vision cannot develop fully without motor development. That is, the two systems are so dependent upon each other that one cannot operate efficiently without the other.

In attempting to discover the role of movement in vision, optometrists noticed that two individuals with eyes clinically equal yet functionally different also differed in movement skills. It was therefore concluded and clinically proven that knowledge of one's environment based on movement experiences within that environment led to greater visual development.

These clinical results encouraged Getman to study children to see if by improving their motor development there would be an equal improvement in their visual development. The results of this research indicated that, indeed, children's visual development could be aided in this manner.

Getman next decided to see how movement training compared with visual training instruments among eye patients needing clinical assistance. After he placed his patients needing the most assistance into visually guided, evaluated movement programs, he found that they quickly learned visual skills they had been unable to master with the use of elaborate instruments. He found that patients acquired depth perception more readily by visually guiding themselves through space than by viewing three-dimensional pictures. Even one-eyed people can develop excellent depth perception through movement by following the same learning pattern that babies follow. Thus, optometrists have found that they can use movement to aid the in the development of vision. They have also discovered a reverse effect that the development of the visual system has had on the general coordination of the patients observed. Many of these patients have become noticeably smoother and more coordinated in their muscular movements as a result of learning to use their visual systems as more reliable motor guidance systems.

One specific visual skill that optometrists and educators alike have linked to poor readers is tracking. Most poor readers have poor ocular tracking abilities (ocular tracking is simply eye movement following a moving object). The problem has been, however, that a great many good readers also have poor ocular tracking abilities. This has led optometrists to conclude that poor ocular tracking is not the cause of poor reading but that both poor ocular tracking and poor reading are signs of the child's inability to integrate muscular movements effectively. Getman (1971) therefore points out the importance of not confusing ocular tracking with visual tracking (keep in mind the difference between sight and vision):

Visual tracking is the total ability to move the eyes across printed words in the proper direction and at the proper speed, scanning a word, phrase, or even a paragraph to glean as quickly, correctly, and effectively as possible the information they contain. (p. 26)

Although these two abilities involve the use of the eyes, they operate at different levels of performance.

Getman agrees with other perceptual-motor theorists about the importance of eye-hand coordination[3] to learning. He points out that although this ability has generally been taken for granted in both optometry and education, it actually forms the basis for the development of visual perception. That is, visual perception is based on the individual's ability to visually guide and evaluate his or her movements through the space and on the ability to explore his or her environment through touch and vision. Thus, visual perception develops through an integration of visual information with other sensory information (usually touch). Children must learn to interpret the environment at close range through touch and taste before they can interpret it at long range visually. The coordination of eye and hand movements, therefore, becomes an important indicator of the child's development of perceptual skills.

Getman uses the example of texture to illustrate this point. If one looks around at the various objects in view and thinks of them in terms of texture, one would probably see objects that appear rough, smooth, bumpy, and so on. On what does one base this judgement? One certainly did not feel all of those objects with the eyes. Therefore, these visual impressions are obviously based on earlier tactile experiences—such as touching these objects with one's fingertips. Over a period of time, by touching and observing such objects at the same time, we are able to substitute our visual interpretation for our tactile interpretations; we gain the ability to look at an object and determine its texture without touching it.

Following this example one step further, we can observe the importance of movement to interpretations of texture. Place your finger on a piece of clothing you are wearing. What does this experience tell you about the cloth's texture? Now gently rub the same finger on the same piece of clothing. You probably found that movement does indeed enhance your knowledge of texture.

What about visual interpretation of size, shape, and weight? Size and shape, for example, are considered so important that every test of intelligence and learning ability contains items about them. We are constantly making judgements concerning all of these factors visually—yet again, what are these judgements based on? Can you imagine trying to determine any of these qualities of an object without previously having had the opportunity to handle and move this or similar objects? In what terms could you describe such an object to another person if you had had no prior experiences with the object on which to base your description?

This points up the importance of experienced-based perceptual learning in all communications. For two people to be able to communicate with each other, they need to have had common visual and tactile experiences, or they simply will not be "speaking the same language."

Getman (1971) makes a strong plea for improved communication between physical educators and optometrists in the effort to reduce or eliminate learning difficulties in children. He points out that optometrists are making a determined effort to

---

[3]It is interesting to note that optometrists refer to it as eye-hand coordination whereas physical educators refer to it as hand-eye coordination.

DEVELOPMENTAL MOTOR ACTIVITIES

aid the motor development of children by encouraging the proper use of their visual systems as guidance mechanisms for both large muscle and fine motor movements. On the other hand, physical educators can contribute greatly to the development of vision through the proper development of fundamental motor skills in children. Getman has, therefore, concluded that the greatest contribution to the elimination of learning problems will have to come from physical educators. His challenge to this profession is quite clear:

> What you do in the primary years can prevent more visual problems and distortions than can all the optometrists in practice. I hope you will realize that you can do more to prepare children for the academic demands now being placed upon them than can any other group of professionals available to children. (p. 27)

CONTEMPORARY THEORIES

Cratty

In his 1979 book *Perceptual and Motor Development in Infants and Children*, 2nd edition, Bryant J. Cratty has made a very critical analysis of perceptual-motor theory. He has concluded, based on the available research evidence, that many of the claims of perceptual-motor theorists have not been proven scientifically. Consequently, even though he believes that movement experiences are essential in the life of the maturing child, he rejects the notion that *all* learning is motor based.

Cratty's search through the neurological literature of the past 75 years led him to the conclusion that Delacato's theory of cerebral dominance is not supported by neurological research. He points out that complex motor actions have been traced to various parts of the brain and are not just controlled by one hemisphere. Hand and eye preference seems to be more of an inherited trait than one determined by a dominant cerebral hemisphere. Another important factor in hand preference has been cultural pressure, such as left-handers being encouraged for one reason or another to switch to using their right hands. Cratty also indicates that having the dominant hand, foot, and eye on the same side of the body, which Delacato deems to be highly desirable, is not common.

Citing child development literature, Cratty also points out that a number of visual abilities develop before the accurate development of many motor abilities. Ocular tracking, for example, may be efficient two full years before the child develops a perfect gait (walking pattern).

Delacato has suggested that in cases where children have "skipped" certain developmental stages, they should be manually guided through these stages by the parent or teacher. Cratty feels that, in cases where this guided movement is done despite objectives from the child, rather than aiding the child, great emotional harm may be done.

In other studies in which investigators have taken children through the developmental sequence suggested by Delacato (i.e., they crawl before they creep, etc.), results have not supported his assertions that such training will lead to higher IQs and an improvement in reading ability. Cratty also points out that a number of medical and health organizations have criticized Delacato's theories and methods as not being supported by research evidence. Cratty concludes that the Delacato theories are of possible value to severely retarded and brain-damaged children, but apparently of little help to normal children or slow learners in reading or other academic areas.

Cratty also rejects Kephart's theory that directionality stems from laterality. He cites research that indicates that the ability to identify right and left body parts is not related to directionality in children with perceptual-motor problems. Kephart hypothesized that children with the inability to translate laterality information into space would reflect this inability in letter and word reversals, thereby handicapping them in reading. Cratty suggests that even if children do reverse letters, it may not be as crucial as Kephart and others have suspected.

Kephart's theory that motor learning underlies perceptual development appears to be contrary to existing evidence that motor learning is specific, or in other words not transferrable to other kinds of learning. Other studies indicate that evaluations of perceptual-motor abilities of young children do not relate to later intelligence (Belta & Williams, 1979; Williams, 1983). Indeed, a child may be as old as 8 years of age before adult intelligence can be predicted with any accuracy. Thus, according to Cratty, Kephart's idea that early motor experiences influence later intellectual development cannot be supported by research findings.

Cratty next points out that Kephart's belief in the importance of visual tracking in academic success is opposed by a great deal of research. Kephart claims that the child's eyes should glide smoothly across the printed page, and if they do not it is an indication of visual problems. Opposing research indicates that the child's eyes move too fast for conscious control and that, rather than moving smoothly, they move in rapid starts and stops across the page. This research has indicated that hyperopia (farsightedness) is more likely to be the visual factor in poor reading than is tracking.

Finally, Cratty cites a number of studies in which the Kephart techniques of visual training and large muscle activities were applied to groups of poor readers while control groups were given reading practice. In each case there was either no significant difference between groups, or the control groups improved.

Therefore, Cratty has concluded that, in general, Kephart's techniques do not appear to lead to improved reading ability in normal children and children with reading problems. He does point out, however, that certain of Kephart's ideas do have merit. For example, he feels that Kephart's motor development program designed for neurologically impaired youngsters could be of value in improving motor functions. That is, certain motor abilities which are specifically trained for through Kephart's techniques do seem to improve. Because of lack of conclusive evidence one way or the other, Cratty stresses that Kephart's theory that motor activities in the preschool years may prepare children for later learnings should not be totally discarded without further investigation.

Cratty is also quite critical of many of the claims of Getman. For example, Getman's belief that movement efficiency is basic to ocular functions and, ultimately, to academic success is not supported by available evidence, according to Cratty. It appears that the ability to read well is mainly dependent on the higher mental processes. Studies have consistently indicated IQ differences between good and poor readers. Therefore, Cratty suggests that because reading calls upon the use of both the eyes and the brain, it is probably the brain more than the eyes which will make the greatest contribution to the understanding of the printed page.

There does not seem to be a great deal of support for Getman's theory of a close relationship between ocular function and reading ability. Cratty cites two studies that found reading understanding and eye movements to have very little relationship to each other. Also, Cratty feels that visual training to reduce the number of times the child's eyes come to rest per 100 words would not increase reading speed. Cratty points out that as children mature, they naturally read faster because they fix their eyes on fewer words. He feels that visual training to decrease the number of fixations would defeat its own purpose because children would have to fixate longer on each word upon which their eyes came to rest.

Again as with Kephart, Cratty points out that tracking ability is not related to reading ability. The number of times a child's eyes fix on a group of words, for example, seems to be inherited and relatively stable as the child matures. He suggests that efforts to train the eyes to function in some other manner appear to have little chance for success.

Cratty reviewed the existing research supporting Getman's theories and found it to be sparse and incomplete. Conversely, he points out that much research evidence exists that indicates that children's learning problems may have causes other than deficient eye function. Therefore, visual training such as that suggested by Getman should not be administered to large groups of children before more investigation into this area can be completed. Certainly no absolute statement can be made at this time concerning the role of visual training in ocular performance or on the role of ocular training in academic success.

To conclude his statement on Getman, Cratty concedes the probability that a number of children with learning problems do have visual problems. Thus, more extensive and efficient visual evaluations in the schools may lead to fewer learning problems. Nor does Cratty rule out the possibility that further research may prove many of Getman's theories to be correct.

Despite criticisms concerning these theories, Cratty recognizes the contributions that movement behavior can make in the lives of children. In his book *Physical Expressions of Intelligence* (1972), he cites research studies and other supporting evidence in analyzing the significance of motor activity to intellectual development. In this book he further explains his position on this topic from both a theoretical and practical viewpoint.

In summary, it seems that Cratty recognizes the importance of motor development to intellectual development, but does not claim that the former is responsible for the latter.

Ayres

In some ways similar to Delacato, A. Jean Ayres in her book *Sensory Integration and Learning Disorders* (1978) states that therapy for learning disorders should follow a similar progression as the development of the brain itself. For example, she explains that "enhancing maturation at the lower, less complex levels of environmental-response function enables a child to become more competent at the higher, more complex levels" (p. 12). She is an advocate for motor therapy programming at a very early and rudimentary level. But unlike Delacato, the programs should thoroughly address and emphasize the body's sensory system as it relates to purposeful movement:

Because many of the symptoms seen in children with learning disabilities subbest dysfunction in the brain stem, much therapy centers around organizing sensory integrative mechanisms there. The brain stem is particularly concerned with gross or total body sensorimotor function, such as that involved in simple space perception or in riding a scooter board. The cortex is better prepared to handle specialized and discrete actions such as reading and the use of tools, including the pencil, but it cannot do so well without adequate function at the brain stem level. Accordingly, therapy emphasizes the gross before the fine and specific function. (p. 12)

Among other things, Ayres seems to be advocating the necessity of being able to master simple tasks before more complex ones can be learned (i.e., the need to be able to crawl before you can walk; walk before you can run; sit with well-balanced and integrated posture before you can write, etc.). Ayres's general principles and methods of intervention for sensory integrative dysfunction include influencing sensation and response, tactile simulation, vestibular stimulation,[4] and other proprioceptive stimuli.[5] Ayers (1978) asserts that "cognitive function has its tap root in the spinal cord, most of the rest of its roots in the brain stem and other subcortical structures, and the cortex assumes a mediating role over all" (p. 12).

Williams

In her book *Perceptual and Motor Development* (1983), Harriet G. Williams explains that perceptual-motor functioning may be thought of as a continuous cycle of (1) sensory-perceptual decisions which are prerequisite to the formation of (2) motor decisions which must occur before both the (3) actual motor or movement behavior, and the (4) information-feedback events that are used to evaluate and/or modify the sensory-perceptual and motor decisions that led to the original movement behavior. She asserts that adequate perceptual-motor development provides children with the means for dealing effectively with the environment. She describes perceptual-motor skills as including gross motor, fine motor, and body awareness behaviors as well as simple perceptual skills.

Although a direct connection still appears elusive, Williams does believe that perceptual-motor development is intricately interrelated with the perceptual and cognitive dimensions of development:

Most recent behavior evidence suggests that there are small but important interrelationships among perceptual-motor development, perception, and cognitive functioning in young children four to seven years of age. These relationships are stronger for four and five year olds than for older children. There is some evidence to suggest that for slowly developing children, there is an important link among perceptual-motor, perceptual, and cognitive behavior, and when one aspect of that development is delayed, other related dimensions of the child's behavior may also show some alteration or delay. (p. 30)

---

[4]Actions which affect the vestibular system, or motion detecting systems in the body. (Ayres, 1978, p. 56)

[5]"Proprioception refers to information arising from the body especially from muscles, joints, ligaments, and receptors associated with the bones." (Ayers, 1978, p. 66)

Furthermore, Williams believes that intra-sensory development is important to overall development. Tactile-kinesthetic systems and auditory abilities are specifically detailed in her book. Likewise, she believes that intersensory integration is very important. Auditory-visual, auditory-tactile, visual-tactile, and other intersensory interactions are detailed and discussed with respect to cognitive development and the development of a spatial reference system. Williams emphasizes that important motor and physical aspects of perceptual-motor development include fine motor control, gross motor skills, balance, and body awareness.

Haywood

In 1986, Kathleen Haywood's book *Life Span Motor Development* emphasized the need for a solid perceptual-motor foundation. Haywood suggests that "almost every motor act in one sense is a perceptual-motor skill" (p. 1960). Individuals combine sensory information with memories of previous experiences and perceive the surrounding world. Then, based on these perceptions, they effect a motor response. This process depends on the development of several areas of perceptual motor function. Haywood especially emphasizes the areas of visual development, kinesthetic development, auditory development, and finally the integration of this sensory information. With respect to visual development, she finds figure-ground, distance-depth, and spatial skills of great importance. Haywood also defines and emphasizes kinesthetics, body awareness, laterality, directionality, spatial dimensions, midline crossing, lateral dominance, tactile discrimination, and balance skills. According to Haywood, auditory localization, auditory discrimination, and auditory figure-ground skills are all thought to be important to auditory development. Finally, she feels that skillful integration of all incoming sensory information is essential, and insists that visual-kinesthetic, visual-auditory, and auditory-kinesthetic skills are essential for successful functioning. In order to address these vital areas, Haywood (1986) suggests that,

> practice with activities requiring a response based on perception of a stimulus helps children improve their level skill performance. The aspects of perception involved in skill performance are many and varied. Therefore, comprehensive physical education and early childhood programs should include a variety of tasks requiring visual, kinesthetic, and auditory perceptual-motor responses as well as tasks requiring intersensory integration. (p. 200)

Payne and Isaacs

G.V. Payne and L.D. Isaac's book *Human Motor Development* (1987) very refreshingly points out that,

> although perceptual-motor is one of the most commonly used terms in physical education, it is also one of the most confusing. Perceptual-motor refers to movement activities used to enhance academic or intellectual performance. Perceptual-motor also implies a relationship between the perceptions and human movement. Although most human movement occurs via the perceptual-motor process, only certain movements are popularly believed to be perceptual-motor activities. Among the movements most often

cited for value in improving cognitive or academic performance are balance, spatial, temporal, body, and directional awareness. (pp. 81-82)

Payne and Isaacs (1987) reviewed the literature on perceptual-motor development and note the modern debt to earlier theorists. Decades ago, Kephart and Delacato proposed theories that have significantly affected education. Both theorists claimed that specific movement activities can improve cognitive or academic performance. However, these claims have been met with heavy criticism principally due to the lack of scientific substantiation. Nevertheless, both theorists continue to have many proponents and therefore continue to have an impact on contemporary education theory.

Even though a direct cognitive or academic benefit from perceptual-motor program has not yet been substantiated scientifically, movement programs which specifically incorporate academic concepts with movement activities may also be excellent indirect ways of facilitating the remediation of an academic weakness and certainly may help supplement and reinforce a child's education.

SUMMARY AND CONCLUSIONS

One very important point which has largely been overlooked is the potential for improving motor abilities of children through perceptual-motor programs. In our rush to connect improvement in motor skills with improvement in learning ability, we have neglected the fact that through perceptual-motor training programs many children with poor motor skills have greatly improved their motor performance. Consequently, if we believe in the worth and importance of the development of motor skills in the growth and development of young children, perceptual-motor programs would be of great significance in the life of the child, even if they did not lead to an improvement in reading or other cognitive areas.

Perceptual-motor theory may offer at least part of the answer to the problem of children with learning difficulties. As Cratty has warned, however, learning theory is only as strong as the research that backs it up. What, then, does research tell us about the applicability of perceptual-motor theory? In Chapter 3 of this book we will attempt to address this question as it relates to all children, exceptional or otherwise.

Children who function below average cognitively often function below average motorically. In many cases, the cause of the cognitive delay (whether it is congenital, physical, or environmental) is often the cause of the motoric delay. Therefore, both the cognitive and the motor areas are "victims" to a common agent (cerebral palsy, for example), rather than directly causing weaknesses in each other. Perhaps, because these cognitive/motoric delays seemed to appear together, or even indirectly interact, researchers in the past have strived to find a causal link between the two; that is, theories have been put forth blaming poor cognitive function on poor motor function even though something else was usually causing both the cognitive and motor problems. These theories expected (hoped) that motor, or perceptual-motor, intervention programs would benefit cognitive function. Not surprisingly, the evidence does not support such a causal relationship.

However, what *has* been shown consistently is that children who function below average motorically, if given appropriate motor intervention programs aimed at the areas of weakness, do significantly improve in their motor skills. Therefore, children who are deficient motorically should have, and can benefit from, intervention programs of appropriate developmental motor skill activities. Any link between motoric improvement and cognitive improvement is at best indirect, but more important it is *irrelevant*! If children are weak motorically, they need appropriate motor intervention programs. Appropriate motor intervention significantly improves children's motor function. The purpose of the rest of this book is to present guidelines to the educator related to the effective implementation of quality motor activity programs.

REFERENCES

Ayres, A.J. (1978). *Sensory integration and learning disorders.* Los Angeles: Western Psychological Services.

Belta, D., & Williams, H. (1979). Prediction of later cognitive behavior from early school perceptual-motor, perceptual, and cognitive performance. *Perceptual Motor Skills, 49,* 131-141.

Cratty, B.J. (1972). *Physical expressions of intelligence.* Englewood Cliffs, NJ: Prentice-Hall.

Cratty, B.J. (1979). *Perceptual and motor development in infants and children* (2nd ed.). Englewood Cliffs, NJ: Prentice-Hall.

Delacato, C.H. (1959). *The treatment and prevention of reading problems.* Springfield, IL: Charles C. Thomas.

Delacato, C.H. (1963). *The diagnosis and treatment of speech and reading problems.* Springfield, IL: Charles C. Thomas.

Flavel, J.H. (1963). *The developmental psychology of Jean Piaget.* Princeton, NJ: Van Nostrand.

Getman, G.N. (1971). Concerns of the optometrist for motor development. *Foundations and practices in perceptual-motor learning: A quest for understanding.* Washington, DC: American Alliance for Health, Physical Education, Recreation and Dance.

Haywood, K. (1986). *Life span motor development.* Champaign, IL: Human Kinetics.

Hebb, D.O. (1949). *The organization of behavior.* New York: Basic Books.

Kephart, N.C. (1960). *The slow learner in the classroom.* Columbus, OH: Charles E. Merrill.

Payhne, P.V., & Isaacs, L. (1987). *Human motor development.* Mountain View, CA: Mayfield.

Piaget, J., & Inhelder, B. (1969). *The psychology of the child.* New York: Basic Books.

Radler, D.H., & Kephart, N.C. (1960). *Success through play.* New York: Harper & Row.

Williams, H.G. (1983). *Perceptual and motor development.* Englewood Cliffs, NJ: Prentice-Hall.

3

The Need for Developmental Motor Activities

Whatever skeptic could inquire for,
For every why he had a wherefore
Samuel Butler

Researchers in the past have looked for a possible relationship between motor ability and academic achievement in young children. As was previously stated in Chapter 1, educational experts have estimated that as many as 4 out of every 10 elementary school children may have unexplained learning problems. Many psychologists and educators point out that children who have learning problems in the classroom may also have poor motor ability. Again, both of these weaknesses may well be the result of another factor, or factors. But rather than trying to claim a motor-cognitive interaction, let's just accept the facts—some children demonstrate both academic and motor problems—and let's start from a practical beginning.

Can children be classified into groups which most likely to have academic and motor difficulties? Yes, in many instances this is possible and helpful. Each child should be individually considered, of course, but generally mentally disabled children, for example, are one group who are most likely to demonstrate both academic and motor difficulties. Some physically disabled children, as well as some nondisabled children of average intelligence who underachieve in the classroom, are two other groups who may demonstrate developmental lags, both motorically and cognitively. Let's take a closer look then at these various groups of children and see what we may find related to their developmental motor needs.

NON-HANDICAPPED CHILDREN

During the first years of a child's life, some experts believe, there may be a relationship between intelligence and motor development (Williams, 1983). In fact, tests of general intelligence for children under 2 years of age are largely made up of motor items. It is generally believed that babies who are abnormally slow in learning to sit, stand, or walk are also usually slow in intellectual development. Likewise, those children who show early development in motor skills often develop intellectually at a faster pace than would a child who shows below average development. Beyond these early years, however, there seems to be very little relationship between intelligence and motor development. Indeed, we must avoid attributing a causal relationship to motor and cognitive function. Often, other factors are present such as good prenatal care, native intelligence, and an enriched environment; or, conversely, there may be poor prenatal care, peri-natal anoxia, or unlucky genetics. We must remember that such a third, external factor is most likely the entity facilitating—or inhibiting—both cognitive and motor development.

Therefore, as motor and cognitive development appear to be more affected by a third factor, rather than responsible for each other, it is not surprising that with older children and adolescents intelligence and motor performance seem even less related to one another. Certainly environmental factors play a greater role than in infancy, as the older child *chooses* to practice either motor skills or academic skills, both or neither. In other words, with age achievement becomes more specific to the particular task and does not necessarily depend upon general motor skills. For example, practicing a general motor skill such as galloping does not seem to directly help the child learning to write to better control the movements of a pencil. Clearly, it would be better to give the child practice in those skills which are specifically needed for handwriting.

EXCEPTIONAL CHILDREN

Mentally Disabled Children

Many motor function studies deal with children who are classified as being mildly to moderately mentally disabled (MMD). There are many different types of mental disabilities. Common types include mental retardation, specific learning disability, and emotional or behavioral disability. Most all of these children share a common need for developmental motor activity programs. Most benefit from methodologic strategies utilizing a great deal of structure, consistency, repetition, and reinforcement. Most demonstrate a general inability to move efficiently (e.g., the "clumsy child syndrome," a term often associated with learning disabled children, as well as the other, mild to moderate, varying mental exceptionalities).

Among other things, MMD children have difficulty in performing motor tasks that call for a specific, ordered, sequencing of sub-tasks. Remembering to execute more than one or two steps of a skill at a time can be frustrating. Accomplishing tasks made of three, four, or more sub-tasks takes good teaching as well as a great deal of practice so that the sub-tasks become more automatic, that is relegated to the lower levels of sub-cortical thinking (cerebellar), and require minimal cognitive sequencing. Frequently, MMD children have difficulty naming specific body parts (memory), locating the left and right sides of their bodies, as well as locating themselves in relation to other objects (laterality and directionality).

Teaching a variety of motor activities in these programs is considered to be an important educational tool for a number of reasons. Successful participation in game and sport skills can help the child have a better feeling of self-worth. Some experts suggest that motor activities help MMD children by requiring thought processes similar to those necessary in various classroom activities. For example, sequencing, as described above, is relevant to both the playground and the classroom. Perhaps learning to memorize the order of acts in a challenge course may help with the ability to place letters in the correct order in a word. However, much more research needs to be conducted to verify these and other beliefs about the role of motor activities for mildly to moderately mentally disabled children.

Generally speaking, MMD children score lower on tests of motor skills when compared to children of the same age but of "normal" intelligence. Such skills include various balancing, locomotor (e.g., running fast) and manipulative (e.g., throwing a ball) tasks, as well as physical and motor fitness tasks such as pull-ups, sit-ups, standing broad jump, shuttle run, and the 12-minute walk/run. Mildly mentally disabled children tend to score about 2 to 4 years behind "normal" children in motor performance. How much of this is due to possible environmental deprivation and how much is due to the mental disability itself are still questions which are not fully answered.

MMD children also score lower than their higher functioning counterparts in skills that call for fine motor coordination. Where accuracy counts in such tasks as target throwing, or following lines in a geometric pattern, they are less successful. In fact, as the fine motor task becomes more difficult, their chances of success with it decrease. However, there is positive support for the belief that structured programs of physical activity can improve the motor performance of these children. This, of course, points out the need for activity, which can serve as an important educational tool for them. Evidence indicates that many MMD children can, with proper help and practice, achieve levels of motor performance comparable to, or even better than, their "higher functioning" peers.

With this knowledge the course of action is clear for the physical educator who wishes to work with MMD youth. The activity program should be flexible and sufficiently individualized. It should contain a wide variety of movement experiences designed to increase individual fitness and skill levels. The demands of each task should be structured so that success is the norm. Copious, positive reinforcement is needed. A well-rounded program of both gross and fine motor skills should be emphasized. Above all, we are obligated to provide MMD children, like all other children, with a high quality, motor based, individualized, and therefore effective physical education program.

Physically Disabled Children

Whether or not a physically disabled child will be motorically proficient will largely depend upon the nature, severity, and time of onset of the disabling condition. In many cases, sufficient exposure to quality motor experiences will enable even the significantly "physically challenged" youngsters to function on an equal level with their nondisabled peers. Experience seems to indicate that the children most likely to have motor deficiencies are those with significant mental, neurologic, or sensory dysfunctions. A brief survey of prevalent "physically limiting" conditions and the related implications for motor activity programs follows.

Permanent Physical Disabilities

Spinal Cord Injury In spinal cord injury, the lesion level, location and completeness will determine the degree of remaining neurologic function. If injury to the brain did not occur, as is often the case, the child should suffer no mental deficit. Sensations of sight, hearing, taste, and smell should remain normal. However, motor and sensory function of the trunk and limbs will be affected at least to some degree. The spinal cord injured child may completely recover, may not survive without mechanical assistance even for breathing, or will fall somewhere in between this range, as is most often the case. Again, the specific functional outcome is dependent upon the degree and location of the injury. Therefore, motor-programming needs will range from those for normal children to those of the most severely disabled children. Obviously, what neuromuscular function is present should be addressed and developed through quality experiences even in the most physically limiting cases. As we shall see later in Chapter 7 of this book, adaptations of rules and equipment are possible and encouraged whenever needed. With a little creativity and concern, we can effectively maximize the potentials of even the most severely physically challenged individuals.

Spinal Myelodysplasia The functional ability of a child with a spinal myelodysplasia (e.g., a myelomeningocele), like spinal cord injury, depends upon the severity and location of the defect. Unlike spinal cord injury, this is not an acquired condition. It is a congenital condition, meaning the child is born with it. The neurological damage is a result of an embryologic defect. Since this defect may often affect the spinal cord asymmetrically, children will frequently display asymmetrical functional abilities; that is, one side of the body may be significantly more or less proficient than the other side of the body. Because there is a motor and sensory deficit overall, and commonly one side of the body is more deficient than the other, it is easy to see that motor deficiencies could arise due to this left-right functional imbalance. It is therefore not surprising that balance and coordination activities are highly desirable for children with this defect. Finally, the very common, secondary condition of hydrocephalus associated with a myelomeningocele frequently causes varying degrees of mental disability. As the blocked ventricles exert pressure on the cerebral cortex, cerebral damage occurs in relation to the pressure. As discussed in the previous section on mental disabilities, a comprehensive, individualized, and effective motor therapy program is certainly essential for these children.

Duchenne's Muscular Dystrophy Duchenne's muscular dystrophy is a hereditary disease marked by progressive weakness and degeneration of muscle tissue. The sign and symptoms usually manifest themselves in early childhood. The disease is terminal, claiming most of its victims between the ages of 14 and 20 years. As the first, observable manifestation of this disease involves gross motor weakness and clumsiness, it is not very surprising that these children are often first noticed as motorically deficient by their teachers. After further medical referral, a certain diagnosis can be made. It should be clear that quality motor activity programs are needed for these children in order to maintain as much physical and motor fitness as possible in the face of their continually degenerating muscular strength, endurance, and coordination. It is psychologically important that activities be structured to maximize a reasonably high degree of success for these children during their inevitable motor control dissolution.

Cerebral Palsy Cerebral palsy is a commonly seen disorder of muscle tone, movement, and coordination resulting from brain damage. Varying degrees of mental disability are associated with about 60% of the cerebral palsied. However, the other 40% of these children are within the ranges of normal to superior intelligence. By the very nature of the disorder, motor deficiencies exist and should be addressed with these children. Depending upon the actual type (such as spasticity, athetosis, or ataxia), severity (such as mild, moderate, or severe), and parts of the body involved (such as hemiplegia, triplegia, tetraplegia, and diplegia, etc.), cerebral palsy can be exhibited by a wide range and degree of expression. These children need experiences in all motor activity areas especially physical fitness activities emphasizing flexibility, balance, and posture exercises. With these children coordination skills, especially visual-motor integration (hand-eye coordination) and fine motor activities are helpful and needed; relaxation techniques have also been found helpful.

Amputations Amputations can be congenital or acquired. A child with an acquired amputation may tend to favor or protect the affected side so much that balance problems and functional asymmetric motor deficiencies may result. A thoughtful developmental motor activity program emphasizing the adaptation of the lost limb to former and new physical skills, as well as enhancement of bilateral coordination skills is desirable for these children. Total self-acceptance is essential and can be facilitated by a well-planned program of challenging, yet positive experiences.

Temporary Physical Disabilities Common temporary physical disabilities include the following four groups. First are spinal conditions like idiopathic scoliosis, Scheuermann's disease (juvenile kyphosis), spondylolysis and spondylolisthesis. Second are hip diseases such as Legg-Calvè-Perthés disease and slipped capital femoral epiphysis (an epiphysiolysis situation, as is Osgood-Schlatter's disease, of the tibial tubercle). A third type is juvenile rheumatoid arthritis. Finally, fourth are fractures, epiphyseal fractures, sprains, and strains.

Basically, the motor prognosis for all of these children is dependent upon how well they are able to adhere to their specific treatment regimens (such as bed rest, braces, casts, medications, and therapeutic exercises). Once the active disease stages are complete, and depending upon the severity of the condition, the time of onset of treatment, and the adherence to the treatment and rehabilitative program, the child may display a wide range of motor strengths and weaknesses.

During the active disease stages as well as afterwards, a motor intervention program is needed. Activities such as target games and handweights can be adapted for the bed-ridden. The physician must clear the nature and vigor of the activities (please see the sample physician permission/referral form, Appendix B). A well-planned, individualized program of motor therapy is essential to maintaining minimal fitness levels and self-confidence, and to minimizing possible physical/motor deficits later on due to prolonged disuse.

Medical Conditions Common medical conditions seen in children are diabetes mellitus, asthma, cystic fibrosis, leukemia, hemophilia, and seizure disorders. A thoughtful program of motor activities is imperative for these children regardless of their medical condition, type, or severity. As described above, motor activities can be adapted to be safe and appropriate for all children, even those needing bed rest. Development of a healthy mental attitude and, therefore, a positive self-concept are principal therapeutic objectives for these children. well-planned motor experiences can provide a vehicle to directly meet these needs. In addition, the physical demands of the activities themselves and the subsequent increase in the child's overall health and fitness status often lessens the severity of the disease. Often, after a period of quality motor experiences, many of these children are indistinguishable from their "unexceptional" counterparts.

Sensory Disabilities Visual or hearing impairments, by nature of the disorders themselves obligate a sensory deficit and, therefore, a sensorimotor challenge.

Depending upon the severity of the impairment and the quality of early intervention, the motor prognosis for the sensorily impaired child is extremely variable. Most motor programs will emphasize the development of the senses that are already intact as well as attempt to remediate the affected senses as much as possible. After a period of quality motor intervention, many of these children are indistinguishable in their actual performance on many motor skills from their nonimpaired peers. Each year, the performances of the participants at the national sporting events for the deaf and blind exemplify this claim.

Exceptional Children: Closing Thoughts

The physical or mental condition itself should not totally dictate the child's "motor diagnosis" or "motor prognosis." It is the individual child and the quality of the motor therapy opportunities made available that will dictate this status. Certainly, the need for quality developmental motor experiences is at least as important for children with exceptionalities as it is for their "nonexceptional" counterparts.

The 1991 edition of *Games, Sports, and Exercises for the Physically Disabled*, by Ronald C. Adams and Jeffrey A. McCubbin can provide the reader with further information regarding the medical aspects of these conditions, including a complete discussion of physical and motor activities and therapeutic exercises for each condition, and an in-depth discussion on adapted equipment for effective motor programming for exceptional children.

RESEARCH IMPLICATIONS

Based upon her review of research, Hope Smith (1968) presented some very readable information for teachers who are interested in developmental motor function and in teaching children. She reminds us that these implications are only speculative in nature, and that they need to be evaluated in a teaching-learning situation using necessary research procedures. Nevertheless, they are discussed here in order to further stimulate thinking about the topic.

Vision

Young children are farsighted until about the age of 6 or 7. Therefore, when working with preschool and primary grade children on throwing and catching skills, some specific steps should be taken. A wall target, for example, should be large enough to be seen clearly. If the child is throwing at a relatively small target, it will probably be seen best at a distance of 6 feet or closer. Items such as beanbags, balls, and blocks are probably seen better if they are not extremely small. Select an object of sufficient size for visual-motor control, of sufficient softness to relieve fear of catching, and of lower air pressure (like a beach ball or a balloon) to insure a slow, clearly trackable flight and pleasant receipt by the child.

When identifying and classifying objects, 3- and 4-year-olds generally rely upon the shape or form rather than upon the colors of the objects. At about age 5, color becomes more important than form. By age 6 or 7, color and shape are used in classifying and telling differences among and between objects. The color blue is favored by both boys and girls, with red and orange as a second choice. Yellow appears to be the color least favored. Knowing this, it may be a good idea to include more variety and complexity in play objects and equipment for 3- and 4-year-olds as color is not that important. If working with 5-year-olds, however, a wide variety of colors could be introduced into their surroundings and toys. This may be a critical time, in which motivation can be increased for motor performance through the use of colors. In the first through third grades, it may be possible to make physical education class more educational and exciting by using a wide variety of shapes and colors in objects used for play.

Figure-ground phenomenon is the ability to visually pick out and see a simple figure or object in a complex background. An example of this would be an outfielder visually following a pop fly ball against the background of the crowd. This ability to find an object in the complex ground is a slow developmental process which reaches its peak in the teens. Both boys and girls reach their top levels of proficiency at about 14 to 16 years of age. Then, however, girls begin a gradual reduction in this ability to about age 20 or 21, at which time a leveling-off period occurs. Boys have a tendency to keep the level of performance they have established at approximately age 14 to 16 until age 20 or 21. Then there is a slight decrease in performance before the leveling-off period. Younger children show less ability than older children in this phenomenon, and girls have less ability than boys at each age level. If children do poorly for their age and sex on this visual task, they are said to be *field-dependent*. If they do well on the task, they are *field-independent*. Poor motor performance by individuals in activities that require striking and catching may be because they are visually field-dependent. The physical education teacher should be alert to this possibility and should select a proper course of action to help those with this difficulty. With the right kind of practice. It is possible to increase one's ability in figure-ground performance.

Depth perception and *size constancy* are learned visual abilities which develop gradually as children mature. Depth perception is the ability to visually determine the distance of an object from the observer. Size constancy is the ability to see and recognize the actual size of an object regardless of other things that may change its apparent size. An example of this might be that once we know what a standard-size football is like, it will still be the same size to us even though we may view it from a distance of 50 yards.

The implications of knowing these facts are important. Having adequate depth perception is essential when performing a variety of motor skills. For children, it is important to offer as many situations as possible which give them practice in depth perception and size constancy.

Phi phenomenon (autokinetic movement) is a visual illusion that gives us the notion that a stationary object is in motion. This can happen if we focus our eyes on an object for a long period of time. In some activities, children may be required to maintain constant focus with their eyes on a specific object or spot. A balance beam routine may demand this. If so, the child should be told to periodically look away from the object or spot just a few degrees to the left or right. This can prevent the phi phenomenon and may help the child perform more efficiently.

Retinal inhibition is the term used to describe the fact that in some cases a person may not "see" an object even though that person may have 20/20 vision. The intent here is not to describe the physiological process that causes this phenomenon to happen, but rather to just mention that it does occur. The teacher should give more than just auditory instructions when giving pupils visual direction cues related to motor performance. For example, after giving the pupils verbal directions for throwing a ball at one of many wall targets placed side by side, it would also be a good idea to provide visual direction by walking up to and touching the desired target.

Audition (Hearing)

Many studies indicate that human babies experience some sound sensations before birth. Of course, as soon as a baby is born, it experiences a variety of sounds which continue throughout the developmental years and beyond. Industrial studies have shown that high noise, heat, and humidity levels in the working environment may be directly related to decreased production rates. Therefore, it is important to create a proper teaching-learning environment in physical education if possible. Indoor facilities should be equipped with acoustical materials, and room temperature levels should be at appropriate levels to accommodate the rise in body temperature brought about by vigorous activity.

Auditory figure-ground ability involves detecting one specific sound within an entire complexity of sound. To illustrate, when listening to a symphony orchestra, a person can pick out the clarinets as they play simultaneously with all of the other instruments. This ability depends upon a person's listening training, which would vary greatly with different people.

The implication for teachers of physical education may be that auditory training should begin early and continue in the activity program. Surfaces of walls, floors, and other objects can be of materials that produce various sounds when associated with different activities. When planned for, these sounds can be used as cues to one's motor performance. The sound of a well-hit baseball, for example, can be one of the first cues to the player concerning the success of his or her performance.

Information related to directionality of sound indicates that people have a tendency to begin their movements toward the direction from which the sound cue was given. That is, if a verbal cue is given from the right side of the person instructing that person to move a body part or parts to the left, the tendency will be to move first to the right before going to the left. Thus, when the pupil is working on a specific direction in which he is to respond, the teacher should be sure that the sound cue is delivered from the direction in which the movement is to be made.

Auditory rhythm perception is "the identification of a regulated series of sounds interspersed by regulated movements of silence in repeated patterns. It also involves tempo and accent (increased amplitude at regulated moments in the pattern)" (Smith, 1968, p. 32). Being able to listen to a rhythm and then repeat it is a complex process involving a sense of time developed through hearing. To further clarify this, consider a teacher with a class of pupils. The teacher could play a record that has a specific rhythm interspersed with periods of silence. This teacher would ask the class to listen carefully to the rhythm and try to "feel it." They would listen to the rhythm again as the teacher claps in time with the rhythm. Next the class could clap in time with the rhythm, while watching the teacher who is leading them in the clapping. An example of this could be clapping a three-quarter time rhythm with an accent on the first note, followed by two more notes within the measure, followed by a measure of silence. This pattern can be repeated as many times as one wishes. At this point, the class is involved with music which has a definite rhythm and pattern as perceived through their auditory and visual senses.

Studies have shown that children start to make time discriminations in music through the auditory mode before the visual mode. That is, they can hear and understand a measure of music sooner than they can read and understand a measure of music. Being able to hear and understand the music therefore aids in helping them later to read and understand it. The physical education program can serve as an important medium for auditory experiences in rhythms, and, combined with motor experiences, can be a valuable asset to the total development of the child.

Tactile Perception (Touch)

In young children the end organs of touch in the skin appear to develop in a cephalocaudal pattern, from the top portions of the body to the lower portions of the body. Receptors in the area of the head and upper limbs develop before the lower limb receptors. The mouth and tongue contain many tactile end organs which the child uses to explore objects during the first couple years of life. The mouth and tongue, the fingers and palms of the hands, and the toes and soles of the feet are the most sensitive parts of the body. Both sides of the trunk of the body are less sensitive than other body parts because there are not as many end organs of touch located here.

Children should be given many chances to explore their environment tactually using various body parts. Educators should remember to include activities that involve the less-sensitive trunk area of the body in their physical education programs. Log rolls, forward and backward rolls, and head-first and feet-first slides upon both sides of the body are all examples of tactile activities for the trunk. Aquatics also can provide many tactile experiences; gravitational force is minimal in water, and the pressure of the water against the body and extremities is very evident.

Providing different kinds of tactile experiences through the environment receives little attention in our physical education programs. For example, few physical educators consider the fact that tennis shoes, valuable as they are for safety, have a tendency to "mask" a child's sense of feeling in the feet. Not only do the receptors on the bottom of the foot serve to signal the child's shifting body weight, but they also indicate differences in surface textures. Thus, having children perform some of their physical activities without shoes can encourage tactile experiences. To provide a variety of sensations, play areas could be divided and surfaced with various textures such as sand, cement, natural grass, plastic, and blacktop.

Balance Mechanisms (Inner Ear)

Motion sickness is an uncommon occurrence in children under 2 years of age because the organic development of the inner ear is not quite complete. The balance mechanisms, in conjunction with vision, the sense of touch, and our knowledge of where our body parts are, help us to understand the relationship of our body in space. During activities which require spinning, such as ice skating, dizziness can be controlled by fixing the eyes on one spot while turning.

THE NEED FOR DEVELOPMENTAL MOTOR ACTIVITIES

Including spinning types of activities in the physical education program and teaching children to focus on one spot can help them reduce vertigo, or a feeling of dizziness. Such activities might include spinning around on gym scooters, or playing various forms of merry-go-round using hula hoops, ropes, or gym scooters.

Kinesthesis

When teaching children how to kick a soccer ball for the first time, the teacher may tell them to try to "feel" the movement. What the teacher is calling upon is both balance and the *kinesthetic sense*—the muscle, joint, and tendon senses that tell us the position and movement of the parts of our bodies. Studies show there is no general kinesthetic sense; rather, it is more specific to that part of the body involved in a skill.

This kinesthetic or "muscle sense" is important when learning a new skill, as a student must be aware of what his or her muscles are doing when performing a physical activity. To observe and test kinesthesis, blindfold a person and, using a verbal cue, direct him or her to place a mark on a target as close as possible to a specific spot. To improve kinesthesis, the blindfold is again useful. For example, if learners practice a skill blindfolded, such as a baseball swing, they will use, and probably improve, their kinesthetic sense.

FUTURE RESEARCH

Now having taken a closer look at basic motor and perceptual-motor definitions, as well as at possible research implications, the teacher should consider some timely problems which are uniquely related to this topic. Theories of motor learning are only theories; they must be further studied and developed if they are to serve their intended purpose. B.R. Carlson (1972) has identified some of the problems in motor-learning theories which need further thought and investigation. As Carlson points out, many tests exist for determining intelligence and personality, but few perceptual-motor tests exist that were designed by physical educators. In fact, of the popular tests in use today, most were designed by psychologists, one by an occupational therapist—and only one by a physical educator. The psychologists used movement as a basis for their test items; however, because these tests were developed by psychologists, physical educators often lack the disciplinary background needed to determine what each item measures. For example, in one test the letters "m" and "n" are placed on the chalkboard for the child to duplicate. If the child fails this task, it could be for any number of reasons. However, only a single score is recorded for this test making it very difficult, if not impossible, to identify the problem and how extensive it may be. This is why the physical educator needs to be concerned about better understanding items such as the stated example, as well as about developing additional perceptual-motor tests.

Another related problem is that many tests today are subjectively evaluated by the person giving the test. This means that a personal judgment is made as to how a child is performing in relation to his or her age. Some people, however, may not be adequate judges because they are not that familiar with normal motor development. A solution to this problem is to develop norms gathered from a large sample of children. Then one child's test scores can be more accurately compared against the scores of many other children who are of the same age. In using such an approach, it will be possible to have a better understanding of the child and the level at which he or she is functioning.

Another area needing more thought is visual perception. Remember that this is more than just the ability to see accurately. Visual perception also involves being able to interpret and make sense out of what one sees. If a child does not have 20/20 vision, this can be helped by prescribing glasses or through corrective surgery. However, there are those children with 20/20 vision who have such problems as reversing their letters when writing or being unable to remember a sequence of numbers or letters they have seen. These kinds of problems cause the child to have difficulty learning in the classroom.

If medical doctors find that there is nothing organically wrong with a child's eyes, perhaps this child can then be helped by the optometrist or the physical educator. Professionals in optometry have been urging the physical education profession to take a more active interest in problems of this nature for years. However, our knowledge has not kept pace with the problems in this area. Physical educators need to know those perceptual-motor activities which are vital for the normal development of visual perception.

The permanence of learned motor tasks is another unknown area that needs further consideration. There has yet to be any study of the long-term effects of this type of training. Just how vital it is for a person to have what is considered to be normal developmental function is a related question that has yet to be addressed.

Another problem needing attention is how the learning of motor skills relates to academic learning. For example, the placing of events in their proper order (sequencing) in the classroom is very important to success. Reading calls for this proper ordering, and following verbal directions also requires it. It may be possible to further this ability through physical activity; motor activities which emphasize sequencing may help the child overall. A series of physical tasks or movements could be presented verbally or by demonstration, depending upon the particular deficit of the child. Such activities may help the child arrange words in their proper order or write the letters of a word in the order they should appear.

In 1975, Public Law 94-142, the "Education for Handicapped Children Act" (as of 1990, known as the "Individuals with Disabilities Education Act" or IDEA), was passed. This law mandates that all disabled children receive appropriate physical education services—including training in the fundamental motor skills, physical and motor fitness, and skills in aquatics, dance, and individual games—within the least restrictive environment. To carry out this mandate, physical educators need effective models for content and methodology.

Data-based instruction and evaluation are gradually being introduced and field tested in physical education. Such tests include Dunn's Data Based Gymnasium (1980), Arnheim and Sinclair's Basic Motor Abilities Test (1979), Wessel and Kelly's I CAN—Achievement Based Curriculum (1986), the American Alliance for Health, Physical Education, Recreation and Dance Physical Best (1986), and others (see Chapters 4 and 5 of this book for further information). Only in this manner can the role and scope of developmental motor activities be fully realized. We need to understand much more about the nature of motor fitness and function in relation to academic achievement in children; what is known about this area, although opinions and findings vary, appears encouraging and certainly warrants further investigation.

REFERENCES

Adams, R.C., & McCubbin, J.A. (1991). *Games, sports, and exercises for the physically disabled* (4th ed.). Philadelphia: Lea & Febiger.

American Alliance for Health, Physical Education, Recreation and Dance (1986). *Physical Best* [Assessment and curriculum program.] Washington, DC: AAHPERD.

Arnheim, D.D., & Sinclair, W.A. (1979). *The clumsy child: A program of motor therapy* (2nd ed). St. Louis, MO: C.V. Mosby.

Carlson, B.R. (1972). Status of research on children with perceptual-motor dysfunction. *Journal of Health, Physical Education, and Recreation, 43*, 57-59.

Dunn, J.M., & Morehouse, J.W. (1980). *A data based gymnasium: A systematic approach to physical education for the handicapped.* Monmouth, OR: Instructional Development Corporation.

Smith, H.M. (1968). Implications for movement education experiences drawn from perceptual-motor research. *Journal of Health, Physical Education, and Recreation, 39*, 28-33.

Wessel, J.A., & Kelly, L. (1986). *Achievement-based curriculum development in physical education.* Philadelphia: Lea & Febiger.

Williams, H.G. (1983). *Perceptual and motor development.* Englewood Cliffs, NJ: Prentice-Hall.

Part II   *Diagnostic-Prescriptive Rationale*

4

Assessment and Evaluation

There are two ways of spreading light: To be the candle or the mirror that reflects it.
Edith Wharton

When finding children in class like Johnny and Mary who are having learning problems, what can the teacher do? With the information discussed in previous chapters, the teacher could try to identify exactly what the weaknesses are so that these areas can be addressed and ameliorated. To assist in identifying areas of weakness, it is often prudent to first conduct a basic screening test. Screening tests are only simplified measures of evaluation—any weaknesses found would then be followed up by more specific and thorough testing by specialists in various fields to determine the exact type and extent of the deficiency. If a deficiency is found to exist, a remedial plan, or IEP (individualized educational program), would then be formulated.

There are many strategies and types of activities the teacher can use with the child both in the classroom and on the playground to help remediate a developmental motor or academic weakness. If the child does poorly on an item on a large muscle test, and this is verified by formal testing, the teacher can consult with others and prescribe appropriate remedial activities. Many possible curriculum packages and ideas are included in Chapter 5. Many excellent activity examples are outlined in detail in Chapter 7. Finally, the appendixes contain further information on available resources and creative ideas for implementing a successful program to address the needs of all children.

ADMINISTRATIVE CONSIDERATIONS

Evaluation of current levels of ability, performance, and progress must be part of every physical education program regardless of the children's age, overall ability, or physical fitness level. Appropriate teaching strategies are contingent on accurate and appropriate assessment and evaluation data. The assessment and evaluation process, however, is only as good as the test instruments and testing procedures used by the teacher.

Uses of Evaluation Information

One of the most important uses of evaluation information is to screen for students who have fitness and motor performance problems that require special attention. A screening instrument should be short and easy to administer but be capable of making an initial discrimination of student ability. A screening tool does not provide information for prescriptive teaching, so additional testing is required to further clarify the problem (as alluded to above). Again, all students should be given a basic screening. Those with deficiencies are then more carefully evaluated by appropriate specialists.

A screening tool for motor abilities should include the following areas of ability assessment:

- Balance—static and dynamic
- Manipulation—throwing, catching, kicking, trapping
- Locomotor skills—running, jumping, hopping, galloping, sliding, and skipping

A second use of evaluation information is to determine the appropriate physical education placement for the individual student. The concept of "least restrictive environment" must be applied in deciding on the best class placement and should be based on sound evaluation criteria.

The third important use of evaluation information is in developing individualized physical education programs. The results of the testing process are used to identify areas of need and are then translated into annual long-term goals and instructional short-term goals.

A fourth and very important use of evaluation information is in the monitoring of student progress. Evaluation of student progress provides both the student and teacher with feedback important to the learning and planning process. Evaluation in the form of feedback about change motivates both the students and the teacher and gives a basis for changing the instructional strategy if necessary.

Finally, evaluation information facilitates the communication process between professionals, within and outside the school, and the home. A systematic recording of goals and progress provides an objective account of the student's educational experience. This type of concrete information makes it much easier to discuss the student's program and encourages cooperation among the different professionals working with the child.

The following summarizes the specific purposes of testing programs as described above:

1. Tests serve as one way to diagnose an individual's specific strengths and abilities, weaknesses and deficiencies, and to assess the individual's progress and development on selected elements of motor development, physical fitness, and physical/motor proficiency.
2. Test results help in developing annual goals and short-term objectives in the deficient elements of motor development, physical fitness, and physical/motor proficiency.
3. Test results can indicate ability/remedial groupings.
4. Test results provide us with a record of growth, development, performance, improvement, and progress for each child.

Evaluation Techniques

The assessment and evaluation process is only as good as the test instruments and testing procedures used by the teacher. A comprehensive assessment program should include

1. Informal techniques including observations of student performance; self-testing activities; exploration activities; discussions with students, professionals, and volunteers who work with students; rating scales, checklists, inventories, questionnaires, and screening activities.
2. Formal techniques including tests of perceptual-motor functions, coordination, gross motor ability, fine motor ability, physical fitness, cardiorespiratory function, anthropometric characteristics, and specific sport skills
3. Tests, examinations, and assessments of experts made available to those who teach physical education
4. Professional judgements of the physical education teacher
5. Information about the instructional setting including alternatives for class placement and class size; interest and capability of receiving teacher; available program support; attitude of the class or peer group; accessibility of the facilities; and modifications necessary to place student in most appropriate program

Content Areas to be Assessed All children should undergo appropriate physical and motor skill testing. Children with special needs are no exception. By definition, physical education under Public Law 94-142 (formerly "The Equal Education for Handicapped Children Act," in 1990 renamed "The Individuals with Disabilities Education Act—IDEA") consists of the assessment and appropriate prescription of activities in at least these three domains:

1. Physical and motor fitness.
2. Fundamental motor skills and patterns.
3. Skills in aquatics, dance, individual and group games, and sports including intramural and lifetime sports.

A SAMPLE SCREENING INSTRUMENT

Tables 4-1 and 4-2 are examples of two very useful informal screening tests, one for large muscle evaluation and the other for small muscle evaluation. (In addition, an index for over 50 formal and informal assessment instruments follow these figures. The instruments have been used successfully in the past and most of them are still available today.)

Table 4-1. Large Muscle Screening Instrument

A. **Materials**

  1. Balance Beam[1]
  2. Playground ball—8 to 10 inches
  3. Chair

B. **The score for each item is yes or no.**

  1. *Balance*—Static   Yes   No   Comments

     Stand on one foot 10 seconds (Examiner asks child to stand on one foot as long as possible. Then child is asked to stand on other foot.)

     Yes if child stands on either foot 10 seconds.
     No if child fails to stand on either foot 10 seconds.

  2. *Balance*—Dynamic   Yes   No   Comments

     Walk 5 feet on a balance beam without losing balance and touching floor. (Examiner asks child to walk the balance beam from one end to the other end.)

     Yes if child walks a distance of 5 feet without losing balance and touching floor.
     No if child fails to walk 5 feet without losing balance.

  3. *Coordination—Hand-Eye*   Yes   No   Comments

     Child throws ball into air (slightly above head level) and catches it after one bounce, 2 out of 3 times.

     Yes if child catches ball 2 out of 3 times when it is thrown in air slightly above head.
     No if child fails to catch ball 2 out of 3 times or if ball is not thrown above head.

  4. *Coordination—Hand-Foot*   Yes   No   Comments

     Child drops ball from waist-high and contacts ball with foot 2 out of 3 times.

     Yes if child touches ball with foot.
     No if child fails to make contact with the ball.

---

[1]If a balance beam is not available, a 2-inch board or a painted line on the floor may be used.

5. *Coordination—Symmetrical*

Child lying on the floor in supine position is asked to move arms and legs to side and return. It is recommended that the word right and left not be used because many children will not know right and left. The examiner may ask child to move arm closest to some object such as examiner, chalkboard, or door.

a. Slide one arm overhead and return.
b. Slide one leg to side and return.
c. Slide arm and leg on same side to the side and return.
d. Slide arm on one side and leg on other side to the side and return.

Yes if child is successful in moving the designated part without extraneous movement in 3 out of 4 of the directions.
No if child moves body parts other than those designated by the examiner in more than 1 of the 4 directions.

6. *Space and Direction*

Child is given verbal directions to move through space in a designated manner. (Chair is placed 8-10 feet from child.)

a. Walk to the chair and touch it.
b. Stand so the chair is in front of you.
c. Stand so the chair is at your side.

Yes if the child moves as designated 3 out of 3 times.
No if child fails to touch chair or stand as directed in relation to chair (in front or to side).

7. *Body Image*

Child is asked to touch selected body parts. This is a suggested list; the list may vary depending on age and experience of child.

Head	Eye
Foot	Knee
Leg	Nose
Ear	Arm
Elbow	Finger

Yes if child is successful in touching 8 out of 10 of the selected body parts.

No if child fails to touch the exact part; that is, the child touches hand for finger, or fails to touch the correct part 8 out of 10 times.

C. **Suggested Scoring Sheet**

Large Muscle Screening

Name _____

	Yes	No	Comments
1. Balance (One-foot stand)			
2. Balance (Balance beam walk)			
3. Coordination—Hand-Eye			
4. Coordination—Hand-Foot			
5. Coordination—Symmetrical (Angels in the snow)			
6. Space and Direction (Verbal directions touching)			
7. Body Image (Touching body parts)			

Summary Comments:

Table 4-2. Fine Muscle Screening Instrument

A. **Materials**

1. Paper and pencil for each child
2. Blackboard and chalk
3. Pattern of a square
4. Sweater with buttons (shirt, dress, etc.)
5. Lined paper and scissors

B. **The score for each item is yes or no.**

1. *Copying a square*

   Yes   No   Comments

   Child is given paper and pencil and shown a square. Child is asked to draw one like it. (It is recommended that the word "square" not be used.) If child is hesitant, examiner should draw a square and ask child to make one like it.

   Yes if square has four well-defined angles and four sides that are approximately equal.
   No if the square is not acceptable.

2. *Buttoning*

   Yes   No   Comments

   Examiner buttons a sweater and then asks child to button it.

   Yes if the child can button
   No if the child cannot button.

3. *Drawing a straight line*

   Yes   No   Comments

   Child is asked to draw a line connecting two dots. Dots on paper must be positioned so that child must cross the midline with one hand.

   Yes if child draws a continuous line crossing the midline of body.
   No if child fails to join two dots, fails to cross midline.

4. *Drawing circles with both hands*

   Yes   No   Comments

   Examiner draws circles with both hands simultaneously at the blackboard. Child is asked to do the same.

Yes if child can draw any kind of circle with both hands simultaneously.
No if child is unable to use both hands simultaneously in drawing any kind of circle.

5. *Cutting between two lines*   Yes   No   Comments

Examiner takes piece of lined notebook paper and cuts between two lines. Child is then asked to cut between two lines as did examiner.

Yes if child can cut between two lines.
No if child cannot stay between two lines when cutting paper.

6. *Touching fingers to thumb*   Yes   No   Comments

Examiner touches thumb to each finger in succession. Child is asked to do the same.

Yes if child can touch fingers and thumb on one hand in succession.
No if child cannot touch a finger or fails to do so in succession

C. **Suggested Scoring Sheet**

Fine Muscle Screening   Name

                                                  Yes   No   Comments

1. Copying a square

2. Buttoning

3. Drawing a straight line

4. Drawing circles with both hands

5. Cutting between two lines

6. Touching fingers to thumb

Summary Comments:

SELECTING AN APPROPRIATE ASSESSMENT INSTRUMENT

The following material is an index to assessment instruments that address developmental motor skills. First is an alphabetical, numbered list of these tests. These numbers are then used to represent these tests in Lists A to E. The lists illustrate how the tests correspond to various areas of need such as content area assessed, grade level, specific exceptionality, ease of administration, and apparent validity and reliability. This index should help the reader identify viable tests for motor skill areas for virtually any teaching situation and population of children.

An Index to Assessment Instruments

1. AAHPERD Test for the Blind
   American Alliance for Health, Physical Education, Recreation and Dance, 1900 Association Drive, Reston, VA 22091.
2. AAU Physical Fitness and Proficiency Test
   National American Athletic Union Office, Attn: Physical Fitness Program, 3400 West 86th Street, Indianapolis, IN 46268.
3. A Perceptual Test Battery
   Development and Standardization, University of Chicago Press with the Department of Education, University of Chicago, 5801 Ellis Avenue, Chicago, IL 60637.
4. Ayers Space Test (Southern California Perceptual-Motor Test)
   Western Psychological Services, Division of Manson Western Corporation, 12031 Wilshire Blvd., Los Angeles, CA 90025
5. Basic Motor Abilities Test for Retardates
   (JFRC Monograph No. 67-1; AIR-ADR-86-2167-FR, February 1967, Final Report), American Institute for Research, 8555 16th Street, Silver Springs, MD 20910; *Also*, National Children Center, Jewish Foundation for Retarded Children, 6200 2nd Street N.W., Washington DC 20011.
6. Basic Motor Ability Test, Revised
   Arnheim, D.D. & Sinclair, W.A. (1979). *The Clumsy Child: A Program of Motor Therapy* (2nd ed.), St. Louis, MO: C.V. Mosby.
7. Basic Motor Fitness
   Donald Aittilsendager, Department of Physical Education, Temple University, Philadelphia, PA 19122.
8. Bruininks-Oseretsky Test of Motor Proficiency
   American Guidance Service, Inc., Publishers Building, Circle Pines, MN 55014.
9. Carolina Developmental Profile
   803 Churchill, Chapel Hill, NC 27574.
10. Centennial Athletic Testing Program
    Canadian Association for Retarded Children, 4700 Keele Street, Downsview, Toronto, Canada.
11. Denver Developmental Screen Test
    LADOCA Project and Publishing Foundation, Inc., East 51st Avenue & Lincoln Street, Denver, CO 80216; *Also*, University of Colorado Medical Center, Denver, CO 80220.

12. Developmental Screening Inventory—From 4 weeks to 18 months
    Division of Child Development, Department of Pediatrics and Psychiatry,
    The Ohio State University College of Medicine and the Children's Hospital,
    Columbus, OH 43210.
13. The Developmental Test of Visual-Motor Interpretation (VMI)
    Follett Educational Corporation, 1018 West Washington Blvd., Chicago, IL
    60607.
14. Doman-Delacato Developmental Mobility Scale
    The Rehabilitation Center at Philadelphia, 8801 Stenton Avenue, Philadel-
    phia, PA 19063.
15. Early Detection Inventory (EDI)
    Follett Educational Corporation, 1018 West Washington Blvd., Chicago, IL
    60607.
16. Elementary School Physical Fitness Test for Boys and Girls
    State Department of Public Instruction, Olympia, WA 98501
17. Engleman Basic Concept Test
    Follett Educational Corporation, 1018 West Washington Blvd., Chicago, IL
    60607.
18. Evaluation Test for TMR Children
    University of Northern Colorado, Department of Special Education, and
    Rocky Mountain Special Education Instructional Materials Center, Greeley,
    CO 80631.
19. Evanston Early I.D. Scale
    Follett Educational Corporation, 1018 West Washington Blvd., Chicago, IL
    60607.
20. Fit N Dex
    Cramer Software Group, Cramer Products, Inc., Gardner, KS 66030.
21. The Florida State University Diagnostic Battery of Recreation Function for
    the TMR
    Jean Mundy, Department of Recreation, Florida State University, Tallahas-
    see, FL 32306.
22. Frostig Developmental Test of Visual Perception (DTVP)
    Consulting Psychologist Press, Inc., 577 College Avenue, Palo Alto, CA
    94360.
23. Goldmen-Fristal Woodcock Test of Auditory Discrimination
    American Guidance Services, Circle Pines, MN 55014.
24. Hughes Basic Gross Motor Assessment (BGMA)
    Jeanne Hughes, Adaptive Physical Education Consultant, Office of Special
    Education, Denver Public Schools, Denver, CO 80203.
25. Individual Motor Achievement Guided Education
    The Devereu Foundation Press, Devon, PA 19333.
26. Kindergarten Auditory Screening Test
    Follett Educational Corporation, 1018 West Washington Blvd., Chicago, IL
    60607.
27. Kraus-Weber Tests of Minimum Muscular Fitness
    Kraus H. and Hirchland, R (1955). *Research Quarterly, 25,* 178-188; American

Alliance for Health, Physical Education, Recreation and Dance, 1900 Association Drive, Reston, VA 22091.

28. Meeting Street School Screening Test (MSSST)
Meeting Street School, 333 Grotto Avenue, Providence, RI 02906.

29. Memory for Designs Test
Psychological Test Specialist, Box 1441, Missoula, MT 59801.

30. Motor Developmental Activities for the MR
Louis Bowers, College of Education, University of South Florida, Tampa, FL 33620.

31. Move-Grow-Learn: Movement Skills Survey
Follett Educational Corporation, 1018 West Washington Blvd., Chicago, IL 60607.

32. Movement Pattern Checklist
Margaret M. Thompson, Department of Physical Education, University of Illinois, Urbana, IL 61801.

33. Mr. Peanut's Guide to Physical Fitness
Standard Brands Education Service, P.O. Box 2695, Grand Central Station, New York, NY 10017.

34. MVPT: Motor-free Visual Perception Test
Academic Therapy Publications, 1539 4th Street, San Rafael, CA 94901.

35. Peabody Developmental Motor Scales
DLM Teaching Resources, One DLM Park, Allen, TX 75002.

36. The Perceptual Motor Attributes of MR Children and Youth
Los Angeles County Department of Parks, Recreation, & The Special Education Branch, Los Angeles City Schools, 450 N. Grand Avenue, Los Angeles, CA 90012.

37. Perceptual Motor Survey
Mathery E. Sullivan, Physical Education Consultant, Special School District of St. Louis County, 12100 Clayton Road, Town and Country, MO 63125.

38. Physical Ability Rating Scale
University Hospital School, Iowa City, IA 52240.
(Physical Best: See #55.)

39. Physical Fitness for the MR
Metropolitan Toronto Association for Retarded Children, 186 Beverley Street, Toronto, 2B, Ontario, Canada.

40. Physical Fitness Motor Ability Test
The Governor's Commission on Physical Fitness, 4200 North Lamar, Suite 101, Austin, TX 78750.

41. Physical Fitness Test Battery for MR Children
Hollistait, School of Physical Education, University of Connecticut, Storrs, CT 06268.

42. Pre-Test of Vision, Hearing, Motor Coordination
California Test Bureau, 2702 Monroe Street, Madison, WI 53711.

43. Project ComPAC
Dade County Public Schools, Administrative Office, Lindsey Hopkins Building, 1410 N.E. 2nd Avenue, Miami, FL 33132.

44. Project UNIQUE: A Physical Fitness Test for the Physically Impaired
    Joseph P. Winnick, State University of New York, Brockport, NY 14420.
45. Purdue Perceptual Motor Survey
    Charles E. Merrill Publishing Co., 1300 Alum Creek Drive, Columbus, OH
    43216.
46. Rail Walking Test for Girls and Boys
    (1949). *Motor Skills Research Exchange, 1,* (4), 34-36.
47. Robbins Speech Sound Discrimination and Verbal Imagery Tests
    Expression Co., 155 Columbus Avenue, Boston, MA 02116.
48. Sensory Motor Training of the Profoundly Retarded
    (1969). *American Journal of Mental Deficiency, 74,* 283-295.
49. Special Fitness Test Manual for Mildly Mentally Retarded Persons (Kennedy
    Foundation)
    And Motor Fitness Manual for the Moderately Mentally Retarded
    Both publications of American Alliance for Health, Physical Education, Recreation and Dance, 1900 Association Drive, Reston, VA 22091.
50. Stott-Moyes Henderson Test of Motor Impairment
    Brooks Education of Publishing, Ltd., P.O. Box 1171, Guelph, Ontario, N1H
    6N3, Canada.
51. The Teaching Research Motor Development Scale of Moderately and Severely Retarded Children
    Charles C. Thomas Publisher, Springfield, IL 62717.
52. The Three-Dimensional Test for Visualization Skills
    Academic Therapy Publications, 1539 4th Street, San Rafael, CA 94901.
53. TMR Performance Profile
    Reporting Service for Exceptional Children, 563 Westview Avenue, Ridgefield, NJ 07657.
54. Valett Developmental Survey of Basic Training Abilities
    Consulting Psychologists Press, 577 College Avenue, Palo Alto, CA 94306.
55. Youth Fitness Test
    (*Now largely replaced by the* Physical Best *testing software program*) American Alliance for Health, Physical Education, Recreation and Dance, 1900 Association Drive, Reston, VA 22091.

List A: Organization by Content Area[2]

1. *Fundamental Motor Skills and Patterns*

1	11	22	35	43	53
2	12	24	36	44	54
5	13	25	37	45	55
6	14	28	38	47	
7	15	30	39	48	
8	16	31	40	49	
9	18	32	41	50	
10	19	33	42	51	

2. *Physical and Motor Fitness*

1	18	39	53
2	20	40	55
5	24	41	
6	27	43	
7	31	44	
8	32	49	
10	33	50	
16	35	51	

3. *Skills in Aquatics, Dance, Individual/Group Games*

   1   43

4. *Specific Perceptual-Motor Areas*

   4 (Perceptual skills)
   8 (Available in sign language)
   13 (Perceptual-motor skills)
   22 (Perceptual skills
   34 (Visual perception)
   36 (Perceptual-motor skills)
   37 (Perceptual-motor skills)
   38 (Perceptual skills)
   52 (Visual perception)
   54 (Language skills)

List B: Organization by Grade Level

1. *Preschool*

4	10	15	26	48
5	11	17	31	51
6	12	22	35	52
7	13	23	38	53
8	14	25	46	54

2. *Elementary*

1	7	16	23	30	36	42	48	54
2	8	18	24	31	37	43	49	55
3	9	19	25	32	38	44	50	
4	10	20	27	33	39	45	51	
5	11	21	28	34	40	46	52	
6	13	22	29	35	41	47	53	

3. *Secondary*[3]

1	8	23	36	42	49
2	13	27	39	43	50
5	20	29	40	44	51
7	21	33	41	48	53
					55

4. *Post-Secondary*[3]

1	27	42	51
5	29	43	53
21	36	44	
23	41	48	

List C: Organization by Specific Exceptionality

1. *Physically Impaired (self-ambulatory): PI*

2	12	20	30	42
3	13	22	32	43[4]
4	14	23	34[4]	44
5	15	25	35	46
8	17	26	36	47
9	18	27	38	52
10	19	29	40	54
				55

2. *Severely Physically Impaired (wheelchair-bound): SPI*

2	15	29	40
3	17	30	42
4	18	32	43
9	19	34	47
10	23	35	52
12	25	36	54[4]
14	26	38	55

3. *Visually Impaired: VI*

1[4]	16[4]	24[4]	31[4]	40	52
3[4]	17	25	32	42	54
8	18	26	33	43[4]	
10	19	27	34	44	
12	20	28	35	45[4]	
14	22[4]	29	36	46	
15	23	30	38	47	

4. *Hearing Impaired: HI*

2	12	19	27	34	44	55
3[4]	13	22	29	35	45[4]	
4	14	23[4]	30	36	46	
4	15	24[4]	31[4]	38	47	
9	17	25	32	40	52	
10	18	26[4]	33	42	54	

5. *Mildly to Moderately Mentally Disabled: MMD*

2	10	17	25	35	45[4]
3	11[4]	18	26	36[4]	46
4	12	19	29	38	47
5[4]	13	20	30[4]	39	49[4]
7[4]	14	22	32	40	50[4]
8	15	23	33	41	51[4]
9	16[4]	24	34	42	54
					55

List D: Organization by Ease of Administration

1. *Specialized Training or Materials Needed*
    A.   Yes

5	19	31
7	20	44
14	21	

    B.   No

1	9	16	25	32	38	45	51
2	10	17	26	33	39	46	52
3	11	18	27	34	40	47	53
4	12	22	28	35	41	48	54
6	13	23	29	36	42	49	55
8	15	24	30	37	43	50	

2. *Administration Time*
    A.   Relatively Quick (less than 30 minutes)

4	13	24	28	35	50
5	15	25	29	45	52
11	23	26	34	48	

    B.   Relatively Long (greater than 30 minutes)

8	20	33	47
16	22	43	52
17	27	44	53

    C.   Variable

1	7	14	30	37	41	51
2	9	18	31	38	42	54
3	10	19	32	39	46	55
6	12	21	35	40	49	

3.

Expense

A. Relatively Inexpensive (less than $100.00)

1	9	16	23	30	38	44	50
2	10	17	24	32	39	45	51
3	11	18	25	33	40	46	52
4	12	19	26	34	41	47	53
5	13	20	27	35	42	48	54
6	14	21	28	36	43	49	55
7	15	22	29	37			

B. Relatively Expensive (greater than $100.00)

8	31

4. *Group Size*

A. Group

1	10	20	26	34	39	46
2	13	21	27	35	40	49
5	16	22	32	36	41	52
6	19	24	33	37	43	

B. Individual

2	7	13	18	24	29	34	43	48	54
3	8	14	19	25	30	36	44	50	
4	9	15	21	26	31	37	45	51	
5	11	16	22	27	32	38	46	52	
6	12	17	23	28	33	42	47	53	

List E: Organization by Validity or Reliability

1. *Apparently Valid*

1	13	34	44
2	16	35	45
4	17	36	46
5	22	38	48
7	23	39	49
8	24	40	50
9	28	41	55
11	29	43	

2. *Not Presently Known to be Valid*

3	14	20	27	33	51
6	15	21	30	37	52
10	18	25	31	42	53
12	19	26	32	47	54

3. *Apparently Reliable*

1	9	24	38	48
2	11	27	39	49
4	13	28	40	50
5	16	29	41	55
6	17	34	43	
7	22	35	44	
8	23	36	45	

4. *Not Presently Known to be Reliable*

3	18	26	37	53
10	19	30	42	54
12	20	31	47	
14	21	32	51	
15	25	33	52	

---

[2]Areas 1-3 are specifically called for to be assessed and serviced for all handicapped children (Public Law 94-142, 1975).

[3]Although these levels are well beyond the realm of perceptual-motor programming, we are providing this information for readers interested in general physical education or lifetime sport skills.

[4]Denotes especial suitability of the test to the exceptionality.

5

Planning the Curriculum

I hear and I forget
I see and I remember
I do and I understand
Chinese Proverb

A well-planned curriculum of developmental motor activities is essential if improvements are to be realized. We must prescribe our motor programs in accordance with the results of our formal or informal assessment tests. The content should be progressive, systematic, and individualized whenever possible. An effective, accountable program is preceded by good overall planning. Assessment results help us prescribe the best content (e.g., what areas to emphasize—physical fitness, balance, gross motor skills, etc.). Assessment results shed light on the most appropriate methodologic strategies. Mentally disabled children, for example, often respond better to a simplistic command style with copious reinforcement and repetition, whereas gifted children often respond better to more explorative and creative styles.) Teachers must remember that after each lesson and unit, the program should be evaluated, at least informally, so that the needed modifications can be implemented expediently to ensure the most success for everyone.

All curricula should have the following ingredients:

1. A statement of goals and objectives.
2. A thoughtful selection and organization of content.
3. A provision for individual patterns of learning and teaching.
4. A program of reevaluation.

CONTENT CONSIDERATIONS

The age of the child is important to consider when planning the types of developmental motor skills to be taught. Also, as the child matures, the need for environmental structure also varies.

In early infancy motor skills are primarily reflexive. Rudimentary motor skills emerge as the child learns to sit, stand, walk, and run. Supervised, yet unstructured, explorative play in a safe environment is more preferable than organized exercise programs for children 0 to 2 years of age.

In early childhood (ages 3 to 5 years) basic, rudimentary motor skills give way to more refined, fundamental motor skills. Children begin to master skills such as running, jumping, hopping, galloping, sliding, and kicking. Their balance skills are limited as they move from relying on predominantly visual information to relying on predominantly proprioceptive and vestibular cues. Competition with others at this age is not recommended and is often counterproductive. Children should not be put in decision-making situations (open systems, changing variables) when they have not yet mastered their basic fundamental motor skills. However, motor programs involving constancy (closed systems) such as tumbling or swimming, where the child's correct response has little to do with the other children's actions, are excellent for this age group.

By the childhood years 6 to 9, children should have mastered their most advanced fundamental motor skills such as skipping, throwing, and catching. Postural and balance skills become quite refined. Balance should be automatic by age 7. Closed system activities such as swimming, running, and gymnastics are still preferable over open system activities such as organized sports, which demand motor proficiency simultaneously with rapid decision-making skills.

By late childhood (ages 10 to 12), children are able to master complex motor skills and use the memory strategies necessary in sports such as football and basketball. If participation in contact and collision sports is desired, children must be matched by physical maturity and skill level, not chronological age. Practices should be less than one hour long and of minimal intensity. Competition itself should be underemphasized.

Clearly, when planning motor programs, we must not only consider the varying exceptionalities of our children, but we must also consider their age. It is our duty to protect the safety of our children. Well-planned motor programs, designed with developmental readiness in mind, will prove to be very effective and rewarding for all concerned.

METHODOLOGICAL CONSIDERATIONS

Methodology is a way of disseminating information. The appropriate methodology may vary significantly depending upon the type of students being taught and even upon the type of task being taught.

Mildly to moderately mentally disabled children need clear demonstrations of the task being correctly performed. They appreciate a clear command style of approach. They need to know exactly what they are supposed to do. They also do better with only a few variables to consider at one time. Repetition and reinforcement are essential for success.

Gifted children, on the other hand, enjoy variety and flexibility. Demonstrations can be kept to a minimum; they would rather be showing you what they can do. Guided-discovery learning and movement exploration are very popular with this group. These children subsist on lessons promoting creativity and problem-solving skills. They are not afraid to think about something and make a decision.

Younger children need more direct supervision than older children. Program content should emphasize the need for more or less structure depending on the age of the children. Open systems of structure should not be presented until the child is sufficiently mature enough to handle the processing of many different variables at one time. Therefore, closed systems of structure are preferable for most children, and certainly for children with mild to moderate mental disabilities. (We refer the reader to an article by Michael Nelson (1991), "Developmental Skills and Children's Sports," in *The Physician & Sportsmedicine, 19* (2), 67-79 for a more thorough discussion on these content guidelines.)

Motor skills should be taught in a systematic and progressive fashion. Task analysis is the term most used to describe the breaking down of a single skill into its component parts or steps. Advanced children can progress with larger steps and at a faster pace. Children experiencing developmental delays, whether due to mental, physical, or environmental reasons, may need to have the steps of their skill broken down into even smaller parts. The teacher must ensure that the steps are broken down sufficiently, and presented clearly, so that these children will also experience success and advancement similar to their more advanced peers. The completion of each skill will take longer for the more motorically challenged children, but these children will experience equal success if motor skill objectives contain more steps. We refer the reader to both Dunn and Morehouse's *Data Based Gymnasium* (1980), and Wessel and Kelly's *Achievement-Based Curriculum Development in Physical Education* (1986) for a thorough treatment and analysis of this subject.

SELECTING AN APPROPRIATE CURRICULUM INSTRUMENT

An index of selected curriculum instruments follow (which closely parallels the assessment instrument index in the previous chapter). As with the assessment tests, the curriculum programs are listed alphabetically and assigned an index number. The various curriculum instruments are then referred to, or indexed by, these numbers as they correspond to various areas of interest such as content area presented, grade level, specific exceptionality, ease of administration, and other curricular characteristics. Unit III will specifically address a multitude of curricular examples (activity ideas with a specific developmental objective) related to all areas of developmental motor learning.

An Index for Selecting an Appropriate Curriculum Instrument

1. Adaptive and Corrective Physical Education
   (Pawtawket Schools, RI)
2. Adaptive Physical Education
   (Bensalam Township, Cornwells Heights, PA)
3. Body Skills (A curriculum designed to complement the Bruininks-Oseretsky Test)
   American Guidance Services, Inc., Publishers Building, Circle Pines, MN 55014
4. Curriculum and Instructional Techniques for Physically Disabled Students
   (Albertson, NY)
5. A Curriculum Guide for Primary and Intermediate Special Education in the Opelika [AL] City Schools
6. Curriculum Instruction Guide for Orthopedically Handicapped
   (Seattle Public Schools, WA)
7. A Data Based Gymnasium
   (Oregon State University, Corvalis)

8. Directions in Adapted Physical Education
   (Department of Education, SD)
9. Florida School for the Blind Curriculum
   (St. Augustine School for the Deaf and Blind, St. Augustine, FL)
10. Games, Exercise, and Leisure Sport for Severely Handicapped
    (Oregon State University, Corvalis, OR)
11. A Guide for the Instruction and Training of Profoundly Retarded and Severely
    Multi-Handicapped Children
    (Santa Cruz, CA)
12. I CAN—Pre-Primary and Primary Skills (Wessel)
    Pro-Ed, 8700 Shoal Creek Blvd., Austin, TX 78758-6897
13. I CAN—Sport, Leisure, and Recreation (Wessel)
    Pro-Ed, 8700 Shoal Creek Blvd., Austin, TX 78758-6897
14. IEP/PE
    Public Law 94-142 (1975). Federal Registrar, United States Congress
15. Individually Prescribed Program of Instruction for Pupils Who Are Orthopedi-
    cally Handicapped
    (Department of Education, SC)
16. A Movigenic Curriculum
    (Bureau for Handicapped Children, State Department of Public Instruction,
    Madison, WI)
17. Project ComPAC
    (David Reams, Miami Public Schools, Miami, FL)
18. Sequenced Instructional Program in Physical Education for the Handicapped
    (Los Angeles Unified Schools, CA)
19. Special Olympics
    (Kennedy Foundation, NY)
20. Teaching Research Motor Development Program for Moderately and Severely
    Retarded Children
    (Teaching Research, Monmouth, OR)
21. Transition, Project
    Ohio State University, HPER, 337 West 17th Ave., Columbus, OH 43210

List A: Organization by Content Area[1]

1. *Fundamental Motor Skills and Patterns*

1	7	13
2	8	14
3	9	15
4	10	16
5	11	18
6	12	19
		20

2. *Physical and Motor Fitness*

1	6	10	17	21
2	7	12	18	
3	8	15	19	
5	9	16	20	

3. *Skills in Aquatics, Dance, Individual/Group Games*

   A. Aquatics

6	9	13
7	12	19

   B. Dance

6	9	13
7	12	19

   C. Individual Games

1	4	7	9	13	17	19
2	6	8	10	15	18	

   D. Group Games

1	4	7	9	13	17	19
2	6	8	10	15	18	

4. *Other Areas (and comments)*

   13 (outdoor recreation skills/activities)
   15 (leisure skills/activities)

List B: Organization by Grade Level

1. *Preschool*

3	14
7	18
11	19
12	20

2. *Elementary*

2	6	10	14	18
3	7	11	15	19
4	8	12	16	20
5	9	13	17	

3. *Secondary*[2]

1	7	11	15	19
3	8	12	16	20
4	9	13	17	21
6	10	14	18	

4. *Post-Secondary*[2]

7	13	19
10	14	21
11	17	
12	18	

List C: Organization by Specific Exceptionality

1. *Physically Impaired (self-ambulatory): PI*

1	4	7	12	15	21
2	5	8	13	17	
3	6	10	14	18	

2. *Severely Physically Impaired (wheelchair-bound): SPI*

1	10	14
3	11	21

3. *Visually Impaired: VI*

2	8	13	19
3	9	14	21
5	12	17	

4. *Hearing Impaired: HI*

2	8	12	14
3	9	13	21

5. *Mildly to Moderately Mentally Disabled: MMD*

2	8	18	21
3	12	19	
5	13	20	

List D: Organization by Ease of Administration

1. *Specialized Training or Materials Needed*
   A.   Yes

11	13	
12	17	21

   B.   No

1	3	5	7	9	14	18	20
2	4	6	8	10	15	19	

2. *Program Implementor*
   A.   Physical Educator (PE)

1	3	8	12	14	17	19	21
2	4	9	13	16	18	20	

   B.   Adapted Physical Educator (APE)

3	7	9	12	14	17	19
2	4	9	13	16	18	20

   C.   Special Educator (SE)

3	7	12	16
4	9	13	19
5	10	14	20
6	11	15	21

3. *Expense*
   A.   Relatively Inexpensive (less than $100.00)

1	4	7	10	16	19
2	5	8	11	17	20
3	6	9	15	18	21

   B.   Relatively Expensive (greater than $100.00)

12	14
13	

4. *Group Size*
   A.   Individual

1	9	13	17	
3	10	14	18	
4	11	15	19	
7	12	16	20	21

   B.   Group

1	5	9	15	19
2	6	12	16	
3	7	13	17	
4	8	14	18	

List E: Organization-Curriculum Characteristics

1. *Scope & Sequence*
   A.   Moves from a simple to complex framework (yes)

1	6	12	18
3	7	13	19
4	8	16	21
5	9	17	

   B.   Does not necessarily move from a simple to complex framework (no)

2	11	15
10	14	20

2. *Parent Education Component*
   A.   Yes

7	16	
9	17	21

   B.   No

1	3	5	8	11	13	15	19
2	4	6	10	12	14	18	20

3. *Peer Tutor Component*
   A.   Yes

1	9	17
7	16	21

   B.   No

2	8	14
3	10	15
4	11	18
5	12	19
6	13	20

4. *Assessment/Evaluation Component*
   A.   Yes

1	6	9	13	16	19
2	7	10	14	17	20
3	8	12	15	18	21

   B.   No

   4
   5
   11

5. *Record Keeping*
   A.   Yes (more than normally expected is needed)

1	7	9	12	14	16	18	20
2	8	10	13	15	17	19	21

   B.   No (none more than expected is needed)

3	5	11
4	6	

---

[1]Areas 1-3 are specifically called for to be assessed and serviced for all handicapped children (Public Law 94-142, 1975).

[2]Although these levels are well beyond the realm of perceptual-motor programming, we are providing this information for readers interested in general physical education or lifetime sport skills.

Part III   Designing a Developmental Motor Activity Program

6

A "Care Study"

And he who has deserved to drink from the ocean of life deserves to fill his cup from your little stream

Kahlil Gibran

Often times it is a teacher who first recognizes, or at least is willing to admit, that the Marys, Johnnys, Billys, and Mikes of whom we spoke earlier in this book do indeed have serious problems—problems that can and do affect their family life, their social adjustment, their academic achievement, and their success in physical or sports endeavors. Frequently, it is failure or poor behavior in school that finally causes the parents to seek professional help. Sometimes the help comes too late, sometimes not at all. Children with developmental motor impairments may also demonstrate many of the following traits:

1. Hyperactivity
2. Emotional instability
3. Short attention span and distractibility
4. Impulsivity
5. Short memory and thinking disorders
6. Specific learning disabilities in arithmetic, writing, spelling, or reading
7. Speech and hearing disorders

A sensitive, effective teacher is one who knows her children well—not just their names and faces, but their needs, desires, wants, strengths, and weaknesses. That teacher uses that knowledge to detect learning problems which may have a solution if they are recognized and treated early in the child's school life. Elementary school teachers are in a unique position to detect these problems early enough in a child's school life that help can be started and a program of specific remedial activities begun.

If Mary is in a physical education class and her teacher notices severe developmental motor weaknesses such as extremely poor balance and hand-eye coordination, the next step should be to contact Mary's classroom teacher and find out how she is doing in there. If she is also experiencing significant problems in the classroom, Mary should be referred to specialists for appropriate testing. And so it begins: one interested person, then two, then three, and finally a whole team of interested people trying to help a child avoid failure and benefit as much as possible from her total school experience.

If Mary is indeed found to have exceptional learning problems, she will be assigned an appropriate team (the IEP team) to design an IEP (Individual Educational Plan) for her. This process is mandated by Public Law 94-145, "The Individuals with Disabilities Education Act"—or IDEA (1990), formerly called *"The Equal Education for Handicapped Children Act"* (1975).

So, who comprises the IEP team? Logically, the members are those who work directly with Mary—her parents, her classroom teacher, her physical education teacher, the guidance counselor, and other specialists depending on Mary's specific needs. These other specialists could be her pediatrician, a neurologist, a psychiatrist, a physical therapist, a nurse, a speech therapist— basically anyone else who is needed to help solve her developmental weaknesses.

When a series of developmental motor difficulties are detected in a child, there may be a multitude of other problems present, thus making the team approach to problem solving a very desirable and necessary method. The team approach method examines the whole child and attempts to find appropriate solutions to as many of the difficulties present as possible. The earlier that the problems are diagnosed and treated the greater the chance of marked improvement, and the greater the chance of academic, social, and physical and motor success.

The rest of this chapter is devoted to presenting a detailed hypothetical case study of a child from an elementary school. In this particular school, there were many specialists available to aid in the administration of the program developed for the child, Jimmy. This study could serve as a model to show how a team approach method can function effectively in a school environment. It should be stressed, however, that this was a rather unique situation and many schools do not have as many specialists as this one had. The average school, for example, might not have a perceptual-motor specialist, but in most cases the physical education teacher and the classroom teacher working together can accomplish the same things. The language specialist described below was concerned mainly with language development, whereas many language specialists in the elementary schools today are concerned with speech defects. Again, the classroom teacher, with a little extra planning, can reinforce the areas of weakness in the normal classroom setting—sometimes on an individual basis, sometimes in a small group, sometimes by the use of an aide (paid by the school), a parent helper, or an advanced upper-grade child for special tutoring.

Once the problems have been detected, the teacher should begin a remedial program as soon as possible. With a little extra planning, a lot of imagination, and the help of others interested in the child, progress can be made—even if the only ones available to help are the classroom teacher, the physical education teacher, and the guidance counselor.

THE PROBLEM

Jimmy

Jimmy's mother was worried. She was getting him ready for his first day at kindergarten. It should have been a big day in their lives, but instead of it being a joyful, happy occasion it was strangely sad and quiet. His mother had been worried about him since the day he was born, for his was by far the most difficult of her four deliveries—long, painful hours spent in labor and finally a breech delivery. In the years that followed, Jimmy appeared to be a normal, healthy youngster, yet his growth and development over the years had been very different from that of his brothers and sisters. He was slower in learning to walk, in talking, and in accomplishing other motor tasks appropriate for his age. His mother convinced herself that these differences were probably due to a slower maturation rate—after all he was the baby of the family—and that it was unfair to compare him to the other children. She had discussed these things with her husband, but he said she was being silly and that Jimmy was just taking a little longer to develop than the others had. Besides, he reasoned, the doctor would have told them if anything was wrong. And so the years passed. Now Jimmy was 5 years old and was going to school for the first time, but, deep inside, his mother knew he was not ready for school. She knew he did not have the basic skills that the other children had had when they entered school. He did not know how to tie his shoes, he did not know his right hand from his left, he confused the names of colors, he could not count to 10, and he did not know the alphabet. Why? she wondered. She had worked with, helped him, but for some reason he had not responded, and often the "learning sessions" were wrought with anger and frustration—she wound up yelling, and he wound up crying. What had she done wrong? Why was Jimmy different? In looking for answers to those questions, she had feelings of guilt. It must have been her fault, she reasoned. Maybe she had not been patient enough; maybe she had not devoted enough time to him. She was not working when the other children were small, but with Jimmy it was different. She had to work to help supplement the family income, so she had gotten a job when he was 6 months old. Whether or not she admitted it, she had convinced herself that it was her fault that Jimmy was not ready for kindergarten.

In school, Jimmy was lost from the very first day. He was thrown into a world of pictures, numbers, letters, colors, and concepts that he could not understand. He was given crayons that broke in his hand when he tried to draw or color, scissors that he could not make cut, questions that he could not answer, and balls that he could not throw or catch. He was confused, frustrated, angry, and most of all he hated school.

THE APPROACH

It did not take Jimmy's teacher long to realize that he had some serious problems. He had difficulty manipulating crayons and scissors; his large muscle movements were awkward, causing him to bump into chairs and tables that the others children moved around and between with relative ease; and he had tremendous difficulty reproducing even the simplest lines or numbers. Colors and concepts such as right and left were presented to him, practiced with him, and almost immediately forgotten by him. His eye-hand coordination was poor, he had an extremely short attention span, and he did not get along well with this classmates.

His teacher decided that she needed more information about him before she could decide what action should be taken. She referred him to the school guidance counselor for testing. He was administered the Slosson Intelligence test, which showed his IQ to be within the low-normal range. On the basis of that test, he was referred to psychological services for further psychometric testing. The Weschler Intelligence Scale for Children (WISC) was administered, and it showed a wide difference between his verbal and performance abilities—indicating that Jimmy did indeed have a problem. After reviewing the results of the tests, the teacher and counselor decided that his parents should come in for a conference.

The conference was held with the parents, the teacher, the counselor, the physical education teacher, the language specialist, and the perceptual-motor specialist. After discussing the problems Jimmy was having in school, his mother realized that they were basically the same "seemingly insignificant" little things that she had noticed since his birth—he just had not accomplished the things that a child his age and of his family background should have accomplished. It was decided at the conference that Jimmy should be taken to the family doctor and given a thorough physical examination to evaluate his current physical status and to search for possible systemic disease. This time the difficulties that his teachers and mother had noticed would be explained in detail to the doctor before the examination, along with the results obtained from the psychometric testing. A second conference was scheduled for a later date to discuss the results of the doctor's examination and to decide where to go from there. Jimmy's parents left the conference with mixed emotions, but they were determined to find out what was wrong, and how and why it had happened. The problems that had been so easily explained away for so many years were now to be examined in detail.

At the second conference the parents reported on the doctor's examination and diagnosis. They told, with some difficulty, how the doctor diagnosed Jimmy's problem as minimal brain dysfunction possibly caused by his traumatic birth. He had reached this diagnosis by pooling the findings of the medical examination, the family history of the child, the scores of the WISC, and the observations made by his parents and teachers. It took some time for the parents to accept this diagnosis and to sort out their feelings and emotions, but the most important thing was to help Jimmy, and they were willing to do anything they could to help.

THE TREATMENT

Diagnosing that Jimmy had a minimal brain dysfunction was only the beginning. A coordinated program with the involvement of parents, teachers, and the physician was begun.

The perceptual-motor specialist administered Jean Ayres's *Southern California Perceptual-Motor Test*[1] and found Jimmy to be well below the standard score for his age group in all six of the tests: standing balance eyes open, standing balance eyes closed, imitation of postures, crossing of the midline of the body, bilateral motor coordination, and right and left discrimination. A program of large muscle activities was designed by the perceptual-motor specialist and the physical education teacher to improve the areas of difficulty. Many of the activities chosen are listed in the playground activities section of this book. Included in the program were such features as:

1. The improvement of basic body movements, inherent locomotor and nonlocomotor skill, and utilization of symmetrical and asymmetrical activities to strengthen concepts of laterality and bilaterality

---

[1]Southern California Perceptual-Motor Test. Available from Western Psychological Services, 12031 Wilshire Blvd., Los Angeles, CA 90025.

DEVELOPMENTAL MOTOR ACTIVITIES

2. The enhancement of the child's perception of body image, the relationship of the body to surrounding space, and the awareness of direction
3. The development of a sense of dynamic and static balance
4. The development of specific coordinated movements including eye-hand and eye-foot
5. The development of manipulative skills using balls, hoops, ropes, and wands
6. The enhancement of the child's natural rhythmic patterns

These large muscle activities were practiced in the physical education classes and were also practiced at home. A student helper from the fifth grade worked with Jimmy on the days when he did not have physical education.

The parents also started a program of motor activities at home using the book *Daily Sensorimotor Training Activities*[2] as a guide for ideas and activities. The older children in the family enjoyed the activities in the book and frequently worked with Jimmy on their own.

The motor specialist saw Jimmy two times a week and used activities from various curriculum instruments (for example, see Part II, Chapter 6). Some of the activities included by the specialist were line exercises, line and form reproduction, discrimination recognition of basic shapes, coloring and cutting exercises, figure-ground discrimination, spatial concepts, and spatial relationships.

The Thomas Self-Concept Values[3] was administered to Jimmy by the counselor. It reflected a lowered self-concept and negative values held in areas of size (physique) and sharing with peers. The school guidance counselor worked with Jimmy several times a week in a small-group setting. The emphasis was on improving self-concept and learning how to get along with other children. Characteristics of such a counseling relationship included the following: verbal exploration of situations and emotions, expression of feelings through drawing and painting, and use of self-concept workbooks.

The classroom teacher worked to reinforce all areas of learning for Jimmy. To address Jimmy's problems, the teacher set up interest centers around the room for him and other children with similar difficulties. She also made up a special packet of activities for him that focused on his special areas of weakness: concepts of size and direction, colors, numbers, shapes, letters, coloring, cutting, and others. She helped him on an individual basis when possible, in small groups, and had many activities that he could work on by himself or with an aide. She also made special arrangements for one of the advanced fifth grade girls to come work with him for 30 minutes each day. A special folder with daily activities was organized for this purpose.

The family doctor was kept informed of Jimmy's progress and was available for consultation when needed. He was in a unique position of familiarity and trust with the child and his family. This remedial program was continued for a period of 7 months with periodic meetings of the IEP team.

---

[2]Braley, W.J., Konichi, G., & Leedy, C. *Daily Sensorimotor Training Activities.* Available from Educational Activities, Inc., Freeport, Long Island, NY 11520.
[3]Thomas Self-Concept Value test. Available from Combined Motivation Educational Systems, Inc., 6300 River Road, Rosemont, IL 60018.

THE RESULTS

Southern California Perceptual-Motor Test. Jimmy showed significant differences in five of the six tests administered: imitation of postures, crossing the midline of the body, bilateral motor coordination, right-left discrimination, standing balance eyes open. Improvement was noted, but it was not significant in the standing balance with the eyes closed.

Thomas Self-Concept Values Test. Jimmy improved 20 Standard Score points above his pretest, indicating significant progress and development.

Neither the Slosson nor the WISC were repeated at the end of the year.

Jimmy's improvement in academic, social, and motor functions was observed by all of the teachers working with him. He began to like school, he seemed content and happy, and he got along well with his classmates. His ability to write, draw, color, and cut improved significantly. His large muscle movements were more smoothly coordinated, and he seemed to move with more assurance and self-confidence. All in all, he improved and progressed in all areas. Some of the improvement was no doubt due to normal maturation, some to the added attention that he received from his teachers, and some to the team approach method of looking at and working with the whole child. Through the team effort, teachings were reinforced by two or three people, as were Jimmy's feelings of personal worth and value.

A detailed report of the program conducted throughout the year was placed in Jimmy's confidential cumulative folder at school. Suggestions were also included for his next teacher in hopes that his individual needs would continue to be met. He still had much to learn, and no one was sure how far he would be able to go, but definite progress had been made and with help from his teachers and parents would continue to be made.

SUMMARY

If through a program of developmental motor activities children learn to move and manage their bodies with confidence and ease, they should then be able to function more efficiently when learning new movement skills. Again, how much of this success will transfer to other parts of their lives is unknown.

What we do know is that for children with developmental motor problems remedial activities should be specific to the actual skills needing remediation. Thus, if fine motor skills are deficient, a motor therapy program emphasizing fine motor skill development should be implemented. Intervention programs appropriately directed at specific areas of weakness, cognitive or motoric, will indeed result in improvement in these areas of weakness over time.

Well-planned and well-implemented developmental motor programs result in successful outcomes for all concerned. It's up to us. Educators can and do make a difference, and we make a difference every day!

7

Developmental Goals and Activities

All experience is an arch wherethro' gleams that untraveled world, whose margin fades forever and forever when I move.

Anonymous

Motor abilities are an outgrowth of past learning experiences and neurological maturation. For the most part, children should be well on their way to achieving reasonable levels of competency in most motor skills by the time they enter school. However, varying maturation rates or lack of meaningful early childhood experiences are frequent and probable factors responsible for developmental motor skill deficiencies in many children. These children need, and can certainly benefit by, a quality program of developmental motor activities. All children should have the opportunity to develop the fine and gross motor skills considered necessary for basic movement efficiency.

Children lacking motor abilities may well be discovered when the teacher administers a diagnostic screening test. Where improvement is necessary, a program of remedial motor activities can be conducted in accordance with the child's specific needs. Figure 7-1 is a summary of the American Alliance of Health, Physical Education, Recreation, and Dance (AAHPERD) developmental objectives of physical education. Their five major objectives—organic, neuromuscular, interpretive, social, and emotional—provide us with a wealth of information to guide us in the implementation of effective developmental motor programs.

For example, the organic area pertains to activities that address children's levels of physical fitness (e.g., strength, endurance, flexibility). The neuromuscular area refers to the learning of basic balance, locomotor, and manipulative skills which will later form the basis for attaining coordinated, efficient motor skills for success in sports and recreational activities. The interpretive area refers to the ability to explore, discover, understand, and use knowledge effectively, especially as it relates to movement skills and games. The social area refers to how well the child is able to interact with others in a positive and constructive manner. The cooperative natures of most games and sports can help facilitate the development of this latter area. Finally, the emotional area pertains to self-concept. Teachers can effectively improve self-concept and self-esteem with the appropriate planning and implementation of motor programs. Motor skill lessons should be planned to insure success for all participants.

These five cardinal objectives are the objectives of education in general, not just physical education. Indeed, physical education specialists and classroom teachers must

The American Alliance of Health, Physical Education, Recreation, and Dance has identified five major developmental objectives of physical education. They are as follows:

—Organic Proper functioning of the body systems so that the individual may adequately meet the demands placed upon him by his environment. A foundation skill development.

Muscle Strength
    The maximum amount of force exerted by a muscle or muscle group.
Muscle Endurance
    The ability of a muscle or muscle group to sustain effort for a prolonged period of time.
Cardiovascular Endurance
    The capacity of an individual to persist in strenuous activity for periods of some duration. This is dependent upon the combined efficiency of the blood vessels, heart and lungs.
Flexibility
    The range of motion in joints needed to produce efficient movement and minimize injury.

—Neuromuscular A harmonious functioning of the nervous and muscular systems to produce desired movements.

Locomotor Skills

Walking	Skipping	Sliding	Leaping	Pushing
Running	Galloping	Hopping	Rolling	Pulling

Nonlocomotor Skills

Swaying	Twisting	Shaking	Stretching	Bending
Handing	Stooping			

Game Type Fundamental Skills

Striking	Catching	Kicking	Stopping
Throwing	Batting	Starting	Changing direction

Motor Factors

Accuracy	Rhythm	Kinesthetic awareness	Power
Balance	Agility	Reaction time	

Sports Skills

Soccer	Softball	Volleyball	Wrestling	Track & Field
Football	Baseball	Basketball	Archery	Speedball
Hockey	Fencing	Golf	Bowling	Tennis

Recreational Skills

Shuffleboard	Croquet	Deck tennis	Hiking	Table tennis
Swimming	Horseshoes	Boating		

—Interpretive The ability to explore, to discover, to understand, to acquire knowledge, and to make value judgements.

A knowledge of game rules, safety measures, and etiquette.
The use of strategies and techniques involved in organized activities.
A knowledge of how the body functions and its relationship to physical activity.
A development of appreciation for personal performance. The use of a judgement related to distance, time, space, force, speed and direction in the use of activity implements, balls, and self.
An understanding of growth and developmental factors affected by movement.
The ability to solve developmental problems through movement.

—Social An adjustment to both self and others by integration of the individual to society and his environment.

The ability to make judgements in a group situation.
Learning to communicate with others.
The ability to exchange and evaluate ideas within a group.
The development of the social phases of personality, attitudes, and values in order to become a functioning member of society.
The development of a sense of belonging and acceptance by society.
The development of positive personality traits.
Learnings for constructive use of leisure time.
A development attitude that reflects good moral character.

—Emotional A healthy response to physical activity through a fulfillment of basic needs.

The development of positive reactions in spectatorship and participation through either success or failure.
The release of tension through suitable physical activities.
An outlet for self-expression and creativity.
An appreciation of the aesthetic experiences derived from correlated activities.
The ability to have fun.

Figure 7-1. *The five traditional objectives of physical education.*

work together to help children achieve their full potential for each objective. For example, based on a child's needs, a motor therapy program can be designed to emphasize any or all of these objectives. As another example, the lead-up classroom activities in this chapter generally emphasize the interpretive objective; however, upon noting the physical demands suggested for each activity or game, it is clear that all five objectives are being addressed. The teacher can easily choose to emphasize any of the five major objectives with the activities in this chapter by simply making changes in content or methodology as needed.

All children deserve as much individualization in their instruction as possible. A little more repetition and reinforcement here for the mentally disabled child, a little added reinforcement and structure there for the emotionally disturbed child, a little more challenge here for the gifted child, and a few more rule or equipment adaptations there for the physically disabled child, and you're on your way to an effective program. Let these five principal objectives guide you in your planning and teaching. Let the activities in this chapter help you get started.

A variety of exciting games and activities are presented to help children develop and reinforce their developmental motor abilities. For purposes of clarity and selection, the activities are divided into two main categories: classroom activities and playground activities. The classroom activities are directed more specifically at fine motor skills and academic skills which can be incorporated into the classroom setting. Major headings include

1. Pre-reading
2. Reading
3. Pre-writing
4. Writing
5. Mathematics
6. Spelling

The playground activities are chiefly concerned with large muscle, or gross motor, development of the child and can be incorporated in the physical education program.

DEVELOPMENTAL GOALS AND ACTIVITIES

In schools where physical education time is very limited, the classroom teacher can help implement many of these activities during some of the daily recess periods. Activity areas are

1. Balance
2. Coordination
   a. Eye-hand
   b. Eye-foot
   c. Symmetrical
3. Space and direction
4. Body image
5. Rhythm

Many of these games and activities are appropriate for both the classroom and the playground and, therefore, can be used interchangeably by the classroom teacher and the physical education specialist.

IMPLEMENTATION GUIDELINES

"Watch me Miss Roberts . . . Look Mr. Smith I can do it!" These words and others like them have been echoed by thousands of school children on playgrounds across the country. They signal a feeling of happiness through achievement which fosters self-satisfaction and recognition—key elements to future learning success. All too often, however, the voices of children are silenced by the frustrations that accompany repeated failure with tasks that may be far beyond their ability for a variety of reasons.

It is essential that the teacher choose activities that are commensurate with the child's developmental level. Although the activities included here are designed primarily for children from preschool age through second grade, they may be used for any child functioning below age expectancy in basic motor skills, as long as any needed age-appropriate adaptations are made. For example, assume that a child has great difficulty in walking a balance board when classmates can do so with relative ease. A screening test for balance further confirms this difficulty. It would be appropriate to start the motor program at the child's level of ability and progress from simple to more complex balance skills. Perhaps a good starting point would be to have the child walk forward and backward on a painted line on the floor. After the child is skillful at this, the next step may be to walk on a length of board inches wide which is lying on the ground. In effect, you are taking "cues" from the child and presenting progressive learning tasks as previous tasks are mastered. By presenting a variety of interesting balancing skills individualized within the child's developmental reach, successful achievement with all its ramifications may be realized.

A valuable teaching method called *movement exploration* may also be used in presenting many of these activities to children. This approach enables the teacher to use guiding questions to help the child realize an obtainable goal. To illustrate, assume the objective is to help a child understand various bases of support that the body is capable of making. The teacher might say the following: "Support yourself on the floor using any three body parts; Find a new way of using three body parts; Can you use four body parts?; How many ways can you use two body parts to support yourself?; If you use two hands and one leg, how many body parts are holding you up?" By using a little imagination, the teacher can structure many opportunities for children to learn a variety of tasks, including basic problem-solving skills. Clearly, basic academic skills can be infused within such a creative, open-ended motor program. Subsequent teacher reinforcement can make this a most valuable and enjoyable learning experience for all concerned.

The benefits of using a movement exploration approach with these activities is found in the noncompetitive atmosphere. This permits each child to work on an individual skill level which may be quite different from the next child's. In this fashion, a meaningful individual level of accomplishment can be set by teacher and child, rather than a group standard which may not be realistic for some children. In effect, the teacher is "building in" not potential failure, but success. Thus, by using the movement exploration approach, not only will all children find their own level of achievement, but all children will be assured of success.

Emphasis thus far has been given to helping those children who exhibit motor deficiencies. Keep in mind that these activities may be used with children who do not display any such motor weaknesses. Since the best instruction on any subject individualizes learning whenever possible, good methodologic approaches (such as movement exploration) and quality objective-based activities (such as the ones presented in this chapter) can be used to help all children reinforce, in new and exciting ways, the channels through which they learn.

The activities presented here will be useful in helping the teacher plan a challenging and meaningful motor development program for all children. Pre-requisite skills for most of the activities consist of being able to follow simple, one step directions. If any activities seem too difficult, they can either be broken down into smaller, more achievable steps; adapted either cognitively, physically, or both; or omitted altogether and replaced by a more appropriate activity. Remedial activities to work on areas of weakness could consist of various adaptations of the activities presented, in accordance with the needs of the developmental objective or skill in need of remediation.

Furthermore, we refer the reader to the section "General Guidelines for Adapting Activities" later in this chapter for work with the physically or mentally disabled. In most cases, activities can be easily adapted. Manual assistance is possible with very disabled children. Wheelchairs can be rolled or turned in place for situations in which ambulatory children walk, run, or turn around in place. Even the most challenging activities can be altered to allow for maximum participation. Even in the most extreme instances, a disabled child might help the teacher give the instructions for an activity. Still we are obligated to ensure that even the most severely disabled children are physically able to participate, on a regular basis and on an equal level. Your creativity and willingness to learn to adapt rules and equipment will help ensure that this obligation is realized.

The activities which follow represent only a few of the varied and stimulating activities available for use. We encourage the reader to peruse the references for further sources, as well as any recent educational catalogs (for example, the AAHPERD—American Alliance for Health Physical Education, Recreation and Dance, or the CEC-Council for Exceptional Children publications). There are many excellent sources readily available, replete with many excellent activity ideas.[1]

---

[1]Here's a relatively new one that looks great: Mary Kotnour. (1990). *Physical Fitness Games and Activities Kit.* Englewood Cliffs, NJ: Prentice-Hall. 285 pages.

DEVELOPMENTAL MOTOR ACTIVITIES FOR THE CLASSROOM

Pre-Reading Skills

The activities in this section can be used to provide children with much-needed practice in moving from left to right, downward, and across the page in new and challenging ways. This type of reinforcement may provide the child with the basic skills needed for successful reading. Such learning cues as "start at the left side of your page and go to the right; follow the line of print across the page; and move from line to line down the page" must all be mastered and understood.

ACTIVITY: Line Tracing

EQUIPMENT: Large sheet of paper with four lines, 1 inch wide, drawn vertically down the page. An "X" should be drawn at the top of each line on the page.

EXPLANATION:

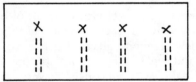

1. Give each child a sheet of paper with the 1-inch wide lines drawn in.

2. Have the child place a finger on the "X" at the top of the first line. "Can you move your finger all the way down the line to the bottom of the page? Now put your finger on the 'X' at the top of the next line and move your finger all the way down to the bottom of the page."

3. Have the child continue without out stopping until all the lines are completed.

HINTS:

1. Young children may need help in locating the "X" at the top of each line.

2. When the child has mastered tracing with a finger, you can place the page under a clear

sheet of plastic. The child can then use a large crayon to trace down the center of each line.

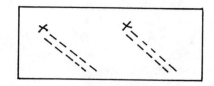

3. Practice in the same manner the other lines illustrated.

Reading

Activities in the area of reading provide children with the opportunity to correctly identify words through games involving movement. Reading skills such as word recognition and understanding the real meaning of words can be greatly enhanced through these games. Specific areas of reading comprehension include identification of words, arranging words in sequential order in sentences, matching abstractions (words) with concrete representations (pictures), matching alike words, recognizing body parts and demonstrating what function they perform, and finally acting out the meaning of a printed sentence.

ACTIVITY: Find the Animal

EQUIPMENT: Word and matching picture cards of different animals. A picture card and identifying word card will be needed for each child.

EXPLANATION:

1. Divide children into 2 or more teams. Give each child a picture of an animal. Teams should be seated and numbered one, two, three, and so on so each child will know when his or her turn comes.

2. The word cards for the animals are in a pile 15 to 20 feet away.

3. "Look at the pictures you are holding; when I say go, the first person on each team will go to the pile of word cards and try to find the name of the animal in the picture. If you are holding the picture

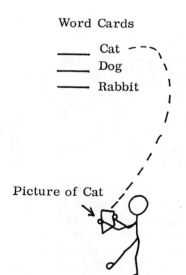

Word Cards

_____ Cat
_____ Dog
_____ Rabbit

Picture of Cat

of a monkey, then you find the card that says MONKEY. After you have found the card, bring it back to your team and tag the next person. Keep going until everyone in the group has the name of the animal."

HINTS:

1. Children should move like the animal in their picture as they go to the card pile.

2. Other things may be substituted for animals, such as modes of transportation, fruits, colors, and so on.

3. The picture cards may be made by cutting pictures from discarded magazines.

ACTIVITY: Run for the Word

EQUIPMENT: Stack of word cards for each group. Numbered cards (1, 2, 3, etc.) for each group.

EXPLANATION:

1. Divide your children into two or more teams. Number the children in each group consecutively. Give each child a card with a number.

2. Place a stack of word cards in front of each team.

3. "Across the room is a stack of word cards. I am going to call a number and a word which you can find in your word stack. When I call your number and word, you are to run across the room and

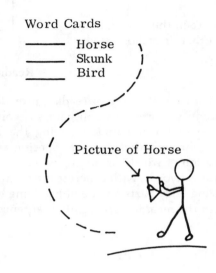

Word Cards

——— Horse
——— Skunk
——— Bird

Picture of Horse

Word Cards

___ Hat
___ Coat
___ Dog
___ Pencil

Word Cards

___ Hat
___ Coat
___ Dog
___ Pencil

Number three— coat!

try to be the first to hold up
the correct card."

HINTS:

1. The teacher may use a picture card instead of calling
   the word.

2. Ask children to hop, skip, or
   go on hands and knees to the
   stack of word cards.

ACTIVITY: Matching Words

EQUIPMENT:

Two sets of matching word
cards.

Red cards	Blue Cards
eye	see
ear	hear
tongue	talk
hand	write
feet	walk

EXPLANATION:

1. Divide the class into two or
   more groups.

2. "I want to see if you can
   match some of your body
   parts with an action they
   perform. What do your eyes
   do?—That's right; they see.
   What about your ears; what
   do they do?—That's right;
   they hear."

3. Give each group two sets of
   cards. "Can you take each red
   card and find a blue card
   which matches it?"

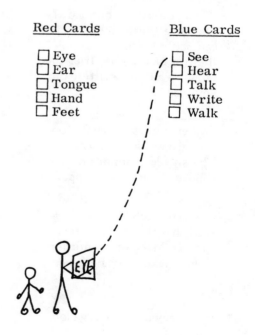

Red Cards

☐ Eye
☐ Ear
☐ Tongue
☐ Hand
☐ Feet

Blue Cards

☐ See
☐ Hear
☐ Talk
☐ Write
☐ Walk

HINTS:

1. The matching word cards may be sound-alikes such as
   deer-dear
   pear-pair
   sew-so

2. The matching word cards may be opposites.

3. This activity may be used as a relay race.

ACTIVITY: Read and Do

EQUIPMENT: Word or sentence cards.

EXPLANATION:

1. Each child is given a word or a simple sentence on a card to act out.

2. "Can you read your card? One at a time, each of you can act out your card while the rest of the class tries to guess what is written on your card."

3. "_____" will go first. Whoever guesses what is on the card will get to go next." This should continue until all children have had an opportunity to be IT.

4. If the child who guesses correctly has already had a turn, that child selects another child to take his or her place.

(The same child)

HINTS:

1. Verbs may used (slide, gallop, jump).

2. Actions may be used (erasing the board, reading a book).

3. Take care that the words chosen are in keeping with the age and maturity level of the children involved.

~

ACTIVITY: Find the Word

EQUIPMENT: Flash cards with pictures of familiar objects such as animals, colors, toys, and so on. A matching word grid should be drawn on the floor, traced in the sand, or painted on canvas.

EXPLANATION:

1. Children may work individually, taking turns, or in groups.

2. If children work in groups, they should be numbered (1, 2, 3, etc.) so each will know when his or her turn is.

3. If working in groups, a separate grid may be used for each child, or a very large grid (each word 3 feet square) may be used simultaneously for four or five groups.

4. "When I flash a picture, run to the grid and stand on the word that matches the picture I am holding. The first person to stand on the correct word wins a point for the team. After the winner is called, go to the back of the line and wait for your next turn."

5. This should continue until each child has had several turns. The team with the most points wins the game.

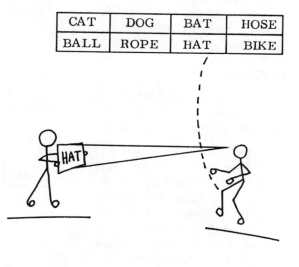

CAT	DOG	BAT	HOSE
BALL	ROPE	HAT	BIKE

1. Scoring may be varied to give a point for all correct responses, regardless of who reaches the grid first. This type of scoring would be most appropriate when an individual grid is provided for each group.

2. For variation, the printed word may be flashed and the child can run to the picture on a grid.

ACTIVITY: Make a Sentence

EQUIPMENT: Stacks of word cards for each child or group of children. Each stack should make a simple sentence when put together.

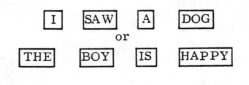

EXPLANATION:

1. Divide the children into groups of three to four and have them sit on the floor.

2. "The name of this game is Make a Sentence. Listen very carefully while I explain how we play. Across the room in front of each group is a stack of word cards. There is one word on each card. When the words are put together they make a sentence like "I saw a dog" or "The boy is happy." When I say 'Go,' the first person in each group will run across the room, pick up one card, bring it back to the group, and then sit down. Keep going until all of the cards are picked up. The first group to make the correct

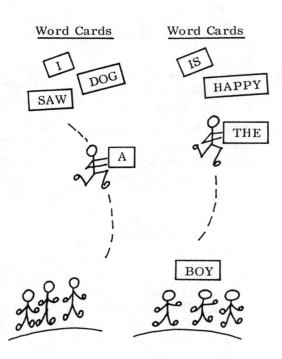

Word Cards   Word Cards

sentence with the cards wins the game. Make the sentence on the floor in front of you."

HINTS:

1. The sentences should be kept very simple.

2. Children may be asked to run, skip, hop, and so on to pick up the cards.

3. This activity may be adapted to smaller numbers of children by putting one child to each stack of cards.

Pre-Writing Skills

We encourage children to exercise their fine muscle coordination through such pre-writing activities as coloring and cutting with a pair of scissors. Children must be able to master handling those instruments in a rather general way before we can legitimately expect them to handle a pencil with enough dexterity to shape individual letters and symbols.

ACTIVITY: Cutting

EQUIPMENT: Scissors with large bottom loop and paper.

EXPLANATION:

1. Give each child a pair of scissors.

2. Help the child hold the scissors in the following manner: the thumb placed in the top finger loop, and the middle and ring fingers in the larger bottom loop. The index finger is used to guide and control the scissors. The child should practice cutting plain paper until he or she establishes the appropriate cutting action. Stopping each cutting

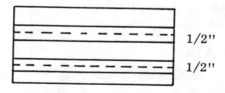

1/2"

1/2"

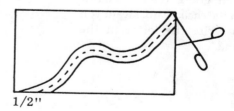

1/2"

movement before the blades are completely closed allows for smooth cutting and prevents the paper tearing.

HINTS:

1. Watch closely as the child cuts; guide the child with verbal cues.

2. Provide cues for opening the scissors and sliding them forward.

3. The scissors should be held in the dominant hand.

4. Once a smooth and controlled cutting action has been established, provide the child with other cutting experiences.

   • Draw lines spaced one-half inch apart across a piece of paper. Have the child cut down the center between the lines without cutting the edges of the lines. For curved lines, the paper should be held and turned in the nondominant hand.
   • Have the child cut out figures (animals, shapes, objects).

Writing

You may repeat any of the following activities for letter recognition simply by combining large and small letters, and upper- and lower-case letters. You can expect the child to respond, for the most part, using an upper-case letter. This added recognition makes the activity a little more difficult and should be done only after the child is familiar with the various ways to write the same letter.

ACTIVITY: Letter Shapes

EQUIPMENT: Chalkboard and open floor space or sand.

EXPLANATION:

1. Have children sit down on the floor or in the sand on the playground.

2. "I am going to write a letter on the chalkboard. I want you to write the letter in the sand."

DEVELOPMENTAL MOTOR ACTIVITIES

1. After the child has had some practice making the letters from visual cues, verbal cues may be substituted. Say the letter and have the child make it.

ACTIVITY: Walk Out the Letter

EQUIPMENT: Sandbox on floor and chalkboard.

EXPLANATION:

1. Children are standing in an open space in the classroom, or on the playground, in a large sandbox.

2. "I am going to write a letter on the chalkboard, and I want you to walk out the letter on the floor."

HINTS:

1. Other methods of movement may be used such as forward, backward, sideways, heel to toe, hopping, and so on.

2. If it is more convenient for the teacher, flash cards with letters may be used rather than the chalkboard.

ACTIVITY: Hear, See, and Find the Letter

EQUIPMENT: Chalkboard and letter grid on the floor.

EXPLANATION:

1. Divide the children into two or more groups with five or six children in a group.

2. "Across the room from each of your groups is a letter grid. I am going to call out a letter and write it on the board. The first person in each group will run across the room and stand on the correct letter."

3. Unless the teacher gives both verbal and visual cues, the child should not respond.

HINTS:

1. This activity encourages the child to look and listen.

2. Variation: Once this activity has been practiced sufficiently, the verbal cue may be eliminated. The child would then respond only to the visual cue on the chalkboard, and vice versa.

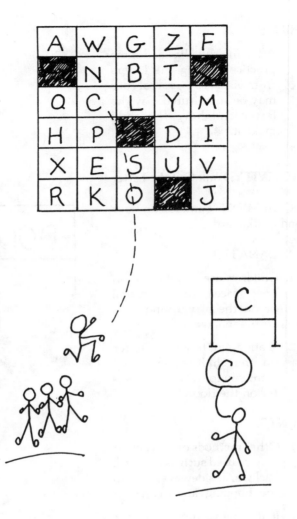

Mathematics

Mathematics activities need not be dull and uninteresting. The following activities are designed to give children the chance to feel, see, hear, and become numbers, symbols, shapes, and concepts. The focus of these skills improvement games is to involve children in a fun and exciting way in the learning of mathematics.

ACTIVITY: Dot-to-Dot Shapes

EQUIPMENT: Chalkboard and chalk

EXPLANATION:

1. Dots are placed on the chalkboard to represent the different shapes.

2. "The dots on the chalkboard may be connected to form different shapes. Can you connect the lines very carefully? Step back. What shape have you drawn?"

3. Each child should have an opportunity to draw each shape.

HINTS:

1. The dots may be drawn on paper and connected by using a large crayon.

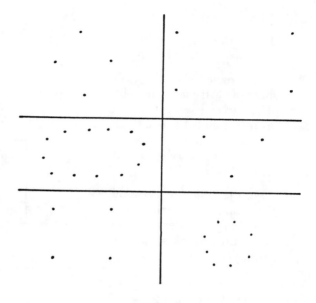

ACTIVITY: Recognition and Discrimination of Shapes

EQUIPMENT: A sheet of white construction paper for each of the six basic shapes (circle, square, triangle, rectangle, oval, diamond). The shape is drawn on the paper about 1 inch wide.

EXPLANATION:

1. Divide the children into groups of six. Each group is provided with a set of the basic shapes, and each child is given one of the shapes.

2. "With your index finger, trace around the shape staying within the lines and trying not to touch the sides."

3. The shapes are rotated within the group until each child has traced every shape.

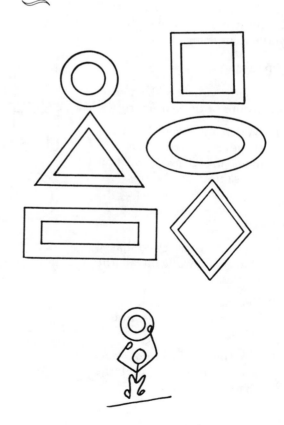

HINTS:

1. Discuss the characteristics of each shape before tracing.

2. After finger tracing, a small sheet of clear plastic may be placed over the drawing to protect it. Substitute a large crayon for the index finger; the crayon may be erased with a tissue.

3. Have the child look around the room, in magazines and elsewhere, to identify and name the shapes he or she finds.

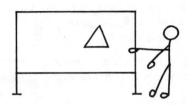

ACTIVITY: Walk the Shape

EQUIPMENT: Chalkboard and various geometric shapes drawn on the floor using chalk or tape.

EXPLANATION:

1. Divide your children into groups of three or more.

2. "Watch me while I draw a shape on the board. Then one of you in each group will find the same shape on the floor and walk on that shape."

HINTS:

1. Be sure each child has a chance to walk on all the shapes.

2. The child can skip, hop, tiptoe, and heel to toe around the shape.

3. Ask the child to find a new way to move around the shape.

DEVELOPMENTAL MOTOR ACTIVITIES

ACTIVITY: Explore the Shapes

EQUIPMENT: Various shapes placed around the room to enable the child to go under, over, around, through, and between them. These shapes may be cut from cardboard, plywood, or plastic pipe. Smaller shapes are also needed as examples.

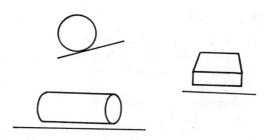

EXPLANATION:

1. Teacher holds up a shape and asks the child to find a similar shape in the classroom.

2. "Can you go over the shape? Under it? Around it? Through it?

HINTS:

1. The shapes must be large and easily recognized by the child.

2. Encourage the child to explore the shape on his or her own.

ACTIVITY: Mystery Box

EQUIPMENT: A closed opaque container with a hole large enough to accommodate a child's hand. (A shoebox with a hole cut in one end works nicely.) You will also need a variety of shapes made from cardboard or plywood. These shapes are usually available commercially in building-block sets.

EXPLANATION:

1. "Close your eyes while I put one shape into the mystery box. Then open your eyes, and put your hand into the mystery box, and tell me what shape you feel."

HINTS:

1. Three dimensional shapes are much easier to identify and are recommended.

ACTIVITY: Do You See It?

EQUIPMENT: Various three dimensional shapes available commercially or made from cardboard (e.g., square, triangle).

EXPLANATION:

1. Make a variety of shapes that correspond with objects you have in the classroom.

2. "When I give you a shape, see if you can find a similar shape anywhere in the room. Can you find a shape like this?"

HINT:

1. Place shapes around the room and have the child try to find them and match them with similar shapes in the room.

Classroom Setting

Table

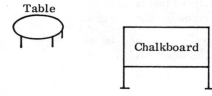

Chalkboard

Globe of World

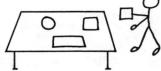

ACTIVITY: Build the Shape

EXPLANATION:

1. Teacher calls a shape, and the child builds it.

2. "Can you build a rectangle?"

HINTS:

1. This activity may be individual or a group effort.

2. Each group may be given a different shape.

3. Fancy materials are not necessary. Scrap lumber, empty containers from the kitchen, many things may be used successfully.

ACTIVITY: What Am I?

EQUIPMENT: None.

EXPLANATION:

1. The children can work in groups of two, three, or four.

2. "Each group get together and think of a number you can be together. The rest of us will then try to guess what number you have made."

HINTS:

1. Some numbers may be made by one child acting alone.

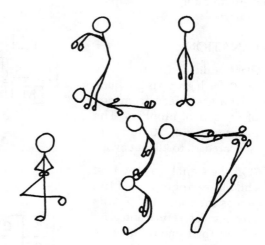

DEVELOPMENTAL GOALS AND ACTIVITIES

ACTIVITY: Move to the Number

EQUIPMENT: A grid painted on the floor. The grid can also be made on a surface such as oil cloth or canvas. It should be sturdy and made with a nonslip backing so it will not slide on the floor.

EXPLANATION:

1. "When I call a number or sign, see if you can find it on the grid and stand on it."

HINTS:

1. You can have the child move to the numbers and signs in different ways such as hopping or skipping.

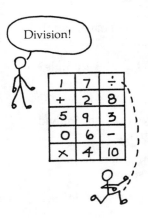

ACTIVITY: Matching Numbers

EQUIPMENT: Two sets of numbered squares for each group of 10 children.

EXPLANATION:

1. Class is divided into groups of 10. Each group is provided with a grid made from one of the sets of numbers. The other group of 10 numbers is located 15 to 20 feet away.

2. "On the signal 'go', the first child in each group will run across the room and pick up any number, return and place it over the same number on your grid."

3. This will continue until the entire grid is covered.

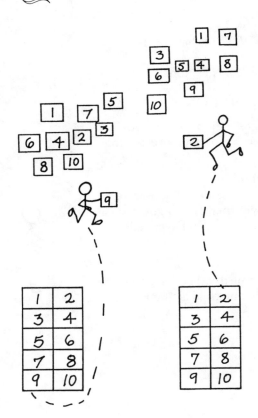

HINTS:

1. Teams may be increased or decreased by adding or subtracting numbers.

2. For variation, children may be asked to hop, skip, or gallop across the floor.

~

ACTIVITY: Find the Answer

EQUIPMENT: Chalkboard and a numbered grid painted on the floor. The grid can also be made on a surface such as oil cloth or canvas. It should be sturdy and made with a nonslip backing so it will not slide on the floor.

EXPLANATION:

1. Place your numbered grid on the floor and have your children sit around it while you explain the game to them.

2. "I will write a problem on the board such as 2 + 2 =? Then I will ask one of you to look for, run to, and stand on the correct answer."

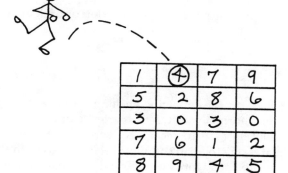

HINTS:

1. You can also use division, subtraction, and multiplication problems.

2. Older children may be given problems that require two grids for the answer (e.g., 9 × 9 = 81).

3. Ask the child to respond using different body parts.

~

ACTIVITY: It's Math Time

EQUIPMENT: A numbered grid on floor. The grid can also be made of nonslip squares arranged on floor.

EXPLANATION:

1. One child is IT and gives the class a problem to solve (e.g., 8 + 2 = ?)

2. "You may be IT first. You may hop on one foot to get to any number or sign. For any number that is a part of the problem, you should land on it with both feet for a few seconds."

1	9	=	7
=	+	8	x
–	2	÷	6
5	÷	3	–
x	o	+	4
=	6	3	=
2	7	8	9

3. After problem is hopped ask, "Class, what is the answer?"

HINTS:

1. Multiplication, addition, division, and subtraction are possible.

2. The child acting as IT should be changed often.

3. Pupil response may be written or oral, individual or group.

Spelling

With the following spelling activities, children have the opportunity to translate a normally abstract experience into concrete terms. Within this activity section children learn to recognize words written on a board and, with the help of classmates, try to form the appropriate words with their bodies. Have them use their fingers to spell words in the sand, and have them play a relay race using letter cards. Other activities are directed toward the improvement of listening skills through games and spelling games in which children must physically move to and touch the letters of a word. All of these activities are intended to help children actually "experience" the spelling of words using as many of their senses as possible.

ACTIVITY: Listening Skills

SUGGESTED ACTIVITIES:

1. Children remain very quiet and try to identify all of the noises they hear both inside as well as outside the classroom.

2. Children play games that use verbal directions: Simon Says, Follow the Leader, Listen and Do (stand up, hop on one foot, hop on both feet, sit down, etc.).

3. Children recite simple songs and nursery rhymes.

4. Children identify animal sounds, weather sounds, and other sounds.

5. Children follow the instructions of a game on a musical record.

6. Children respond by imitating a series of hand claps, foot stomps, finger snaps or combination of each: 2 claps, 3 stomps, 2 claps; or 1 stomp, 2 snaps, 2 stomps.

7. Children close eyes and try to identify common sounds made by teacher: closing door, sliding chair, tapping pencil, and so on.

8. Children imitate human sounds: crying, laughing, singing, or talking.

9. Children imitate weather sounds: wind, thunder, or other sounds.

10. Sounds are made on several rhythm instruments (drum, blocks, triangle, bell, etc.) as children watch. Children close eyes and try to identify the sounds as they are played one at a time. Next, two instruments can be played, and children can identify the first and last played.

ACTIVITY: Body Spelling

EQUIPMENT: Chalkboard and open floor space.

EXPLANATION:

1. Divide your children into groups of three or more, and arrange so they have open floor space.

2. "I am going to write a word on the board. Using your bodies, I want you to form the letters on the floor."

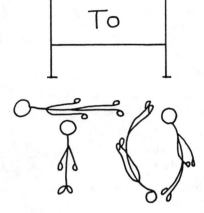

HINTS:

1. The size of the groups and the length of the words may be increased after the children have had sufficient practice.

2. Teacher may call the word verbally rather than writing it.

ACTIVITY: Spell With a Beanbag

EQUIPMENT: Letter grid, beanbag, or similar object that can be pushed with the feet (the grid should contain all letters of the alphabet).

EXPLANATION:

1. Each child may work alone at a grid, or children may be divided into small groups.

2. "We are going to use your grid to let you spell. When I pronounce a word, push your beanbag to the first letter, and touch the letter with your hand. Continue on to the second letter with your beanbag, touching it with your hand. Continue this until the word is spelled."

HINTS

1. If more than one child is spelling, an observing child may be used to check the accuracy of the spelling.

2. Variation: A word may be written on the chalkboard by

DEVELOPMENTAL MOTOR ACTIVITIES

the teacher. A child then spells the word by moving to the appropriate letters on the grid. Care must be taken that there are sufficient letters on the grid to spell the word chosen.

3. Variation: Teacher calls letter sound, and child runs to identify the letter that makes the sound. Some letters may be used more than once as they have different sounds.

4. Use different ways of moving on the grid.

DEVELOPMENTAL MOTOR ACTIVITIES FOR THE PLAYGROUND

Balance

Balance is the ability to maintain your body in a stationary position, either in a static or dynamic state. Standing on one leg is an example of static balance, and jumping on one foot across the room illustrates dynamic balance. Balance is one of the basic blocks upon which almost all physical education activities are built. Success in games, sport, and dance depends, in part, on one's ability to maintain proper balance.

Developing good balance is very important for children. It aids in acquiring smoothly coordinated and well-controlled movements, which allow them to move with self-assurance—an important element in improving chances of success during playground and classroom activities.

~

ACTIVITY: Move and Freeze

EQUIPMENT: None

EXPLANATION:

1. Children should be spread out over entire area.

2. "Can you walk very slowly all over the court without touching anyone? Remember to move to the open spaces and to freeze in a balanced position when the whistle blows?"

DEVELOPMENTAL GOALS AND ACTIVITIES

HINTS:

Ask children to walk

- on tiptoes,
- on heels,
- fast,
- lightly,
- heavy like an elephant,
- with long steps,
- backwards,
- sideways, or
- forward.

Ask children to freeze when the whistle blows balanced on

- one body part,
- two body parts,
- three body parts, or
- four body parts.

Ask children to run, skip, hop, slide, gallop, leap, or jump using many of the variations. Other variations are limitless, but here are a few suggestions not listed above:

When asked to run,

- run like a deer,
- run in a straight line, or
- run in a zig-zag line.

When asked to hop,

- hop as high as they can,
- take short hops,
- take long hops, or
- hop on one foot.

When asked to skip,

- skip raising their knees very high,
- skip around their partner, or
- skip as if they are jumping a rope.

When asked to leap,

- leap from their right foot,
- leap from their left foot,
- run and leap, or
- leap over a line or small obstacle.

When asked to jump,

- jump like a frog from one lily pad to another, or
- jump over a small box.

ACTIVITY: Balance on Body Parts

EQUIPMENT: None

EXPLANATION:

1. "Can you balance on four parts of your body while we count to 10? Can you balance on four different parts?"

HINTS:

Variations include balancing on

- knees and hands,
- knees and elbows, or
- feet and hands.

2. "Can you balance on three body parts while we count to 10? What other three parts can you balance on?"

HINTS:

Variations include balancing on

- 2 knees and 1 hand,
- 2 hands and 1 knee,
- 1 foot and 2 hands,
- head and knees,
- head and feet (only on mat), or
- 1 elbow and 2 knees.

3. "Can you balance on two body parts while we count to 10? Can you balance on two different parts? What other two parts can you balance on?"

HINTS:

Variations include balancing on

- feet,
- knees,

- hands (on mat, and with spotter),
- 1 hand and 1 foot (same and opposite sides),
- 1 knee and 1 hand (same and opposite sides), or
- head and knee (on mat).

4. "Can you balance on one body part while we count to 5? What other part can you balance on? Can you think of another part?" Repeat the same, but count to 10.

HINTS:

Variations include balancing on the

- right foot,
- left foot,
- right knee,
- left knee, or
- seat.

5. "Can you balance on four body parts while you move around the room? Change to four different body parts?"

6. "Can you balance on three body parts while you move around the room?"

7. "Can you balance on two body parts while you move?"

8. "Can you balance on one body part and still move around the room?"

ACTIVITY: Walking a Tightrope

EQUIPMENT: Line or tape on floor.

EXPLANATION:

1. "Let's pretend you are a tightrope walker in a circus. The tightrope is high in the air, so you must be careful not to fall off. Put one foot right in front of the other one, use

DEVELOPMENTAL MOTOR ACTIVITIES

your arms to help you balance, and walk all the way to
the end of the tightrope. Now
let's turn and walk back."

ACTIVITY: Balance Beam

EQUIPMENT: One balance beam (2" × 4" × 8') for three to four children

EXPLANATION:

1. "Have you ever seen a bird balancing and walking on a wire, or a squirrel balancing and walking on a tree limb? Let's see if you can balance and walk like a bird or squir-rel on this balance beam."

2. "Can you walk forward to the end of the balance beam without falling off? Re-member to use your arms to help you balance and to look at the end of the beam as you walk."

HINTS:

- Teacher may want to have children walk a line on the floor first.
- A long board lying flat on the floor may be another necessary progression.
- The 4-inch side of the beam should be used first; as children progress, the 2-inch side may be used.

3. "Can you walk sideways to the end of the beam? Use your arms to help you bal-ance."

HINTS:

- The teacher may want to use the same progression as in #2 above.
- Children should lead first with the right side and then with the left.

4. "Can you walk backwards to the end of the beam?"

HINTS:

- Same progression as in #2 above may be used.
- Teacher may want to hold the child's hand and walk beside the beam or let the child put a hand on the teacher's arm as they walk.

5. "Can you walk to the end of the beam, turn around without falling off, and walk back?"

HINTS:

- Use the same progression as in #2 above.
- Encourage child to turn on the balls of the feet.

6. "Can you carry a ball in your right hand while you walk to the end of the beam?"

HINTS:

- Use the same progression as in #2 above.
- Do the same with left hand.
- Do the same with ball in each hand.
- Substitute different objects of different weights (beanbags, blocks, heavier balls, yarn balls, etc.).
- Put object on floor at midpoint of beam. Child walks to center, stoops, picks up the object, and walks to end of beam.

ACTIVITY: Stork Stand

EQUIPMENT: None.

EXPLANATION:

1. "What is a stork?" (Explain if they do not know.)

2. "Can you stand on your right foot like a stork?"

3. "Can you stand on your left foot?"

4. "Stand on your right foot, and see if you can count to 10 before you put your left foot down."

5. Child does the same with left foot.

6. "Can you close your eyes and still stand very still on your right foot like a stork?"

7. Child does the same on left foot.

∽

ACTIVITY: The Grasshopper

EQUIPMENT: Picture of a grasshopper or a live one in a jar.

EXPLANATION:

1. "Have you ever seen a grasshopper?

2. "Show me how a grasshopper jumps up and down."

3. "Not let us pretend our grasshopper has only one leg. How would it jump then?"

4. "Can you move across the floor like a grasshopper?"

∽

ACTIVITY: High Kicking

EQUIPMENT: None.

EXPLANATION:

1. "Hold one arm out in front of you. Can you kick your foot up and touch your hand? Remember to keep your arm up when you try this. Now, try kicking with your other foot."

ACTIVITY: Donkey Kick

EQUIPMENT: Mat

EXPLANATION:

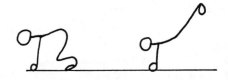

1. "Have you ever seen a donkey kick his back legs up in the air?"

2. "Put your hands on the mat and see if you can kick your feet up like a donkey. Come down quickly after you kick your feet."

ACTIVITY: Spin the Top

EQUIPMENT: None.

EXPLANATION:

1. "Have you ever played with a top?" Explain how this works by showing a picture or bringing a top to class.

2. "See if you can jump straight up into the air and land in a balanced position."

3. "Hold up your right hand. Can you jump straight up and turn to the right while you are still in the air?" Try the same with left hand.

4. Teacher should stand facing children. "Can you jump and turn so that you land with your side to me? Freeze when you land. Can you jump and turn so that you land with your back to me? Freeze when you land. Jump and turn so that you land with your other side to me. Freeze. Can you jump and turn so that you land facing me?"

DEVELOPMENTAL MOTOR ACTIVITIES

HINTS:

- Structures or environmental objects may be used, such as land facing the school or land facing the field, the tree, or the fence.
- With older children, fractions may be used: 1/4 turn, 1/2 turn, or 3/4 turn.

5. "Can you jump and turn in a complete circle before you land? Remember, you should land facing in the same direction as when you started the jump."

HINTS:

- Encourage children to use their arms to help them turn, as well as for balance when landing, to bend the knees when they land, and to keep their feet spread slightly when they land.

~

ACTIVITY: "V" Seat

EQUIPMENT: None.

EXPLANATION:

1. "Sit down. Can you make a "V" with your hands? Can you raise your legs off the floor making a "V" with your body and your legs?"

HINTS:

- Child may place hands on floor for balance.
- If children can maintain this position, the next step is to ask them to grasp their knees to help them in balancing without using the hands for support.
- Legs should be as nearly vertical as possible

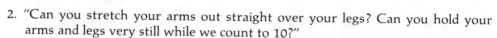

2. "Can you stretch your arms out straight over your legs? Can you hold your arms and legs very still while we count to 10?"

3. "Move your arms out to your side. Can you pretend you are a butterfly? Can you move your arms up and down?"

HINT:

- Ask the children to lean to the right or left as they maintain their balance.
- Some children will enjoy spreading arms and legs as they balance.

ACTIVITY: Shoulder Balance

EQUIPMENT: None.

EXPLANATION:

1. "Lie down on your backs, using your hands to support your hips."

2. "Can you raise your legs up in the air?"

HINTS:

- Child should keep elbows and upper arms in contact with floor.

3. "Can you hold your legs very still while we count to 10?"

4. "Pretend you are riding a bicycle upside down. Can you pedal your bicycle first with one leg and then with the other? Can you make your bicycle go very slow, or fast? How would you pedal your bicycle if you were going up a very high hill? Can you make your bicycle go backwards?"

ACTIVITY: Ball Balance

EQUIPMENT: Large rubber balls.

EXPLANATION:

1. "Put your ball on the floor in front of you. Can you balance on your stomach on top of the ball? Put your hands on the floor to help you balance."

HINTS:

- The size of the balls used will depend on the size of the children.

2. "Can you balance on your stomach without using your hands?"

ACTIVITY: Balance Board

EQUIPMENT: Balance boards.

EXPLANATION:

1. "Stand with your feet on either side of the balance board. Can you lean so that the board tilts forward? Now regain your balance so you are standing straight."

HINTS:

- Use spotters for young children.
- Start with large supports under balance boards, and progress to smaller supports.

2. "Can you lean so that the board tilts to the right? Now regain your balance so you are standing straight again."

HINTS:

- Have child lean backward.

- Have child lean to the left.

3. "Balance on your board so that it does not tilt. Once you are balanced, stand very still. Can you touch your head with your hands while balancing?"

HINTS:

- Children could be asked to touch their nose, ears, eyes, mouth, chin, shoulders, elbows, hips, knees, toes, neck, back, or stomach.

4. "Move your feet very carefully to the center of the board. Can you balance on one foot without tilting the board? Try your other foot. Remember to move very slowly and very carefully."

HINTS:

- Spotters should be used for this activity.

Coordination

Coordination is the harmonious functioning of the muscles in a skilled movement pattern. This skilled movement may involve primarily eye-foot coordination (kicking a ball), eye-hand coordination (throwing a ball at a target), symmetrical coordination (integration of both sides of the body as in a golf swing), or overall coordination (swimming).

Good coordination is essential to successful performance in games, sport and dance. Of course, those movements which are more complex call for a greater degree of coordination. Remember that in order to produce a well-coordinated movement, the specific skills involved must be practiced many times.

Children can develop greater movement efficiency by practicing all types of coordination skills involving parts of, or the entire body.

The success of many classroom activities depends upon how well children can make their eyes and hands work together. Examples are writing in a straight line, coloring within the lines, or cutting with scissors. Children need repeated opportunities to practice those skills developing proper eye-hand coordination, which is so important for learning success.

Coordination: Eye-Hand

ACTIVITY: Jump for the Wash

EQUIPMENT: Strips of cloth of different lengths attached to a strong cord. The cord may be strung between two standards or from one wall to another.

EXPLANATION:

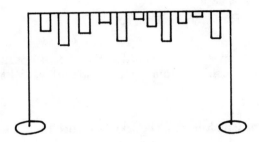

1. "Stand under the clothes line. Now jump up and see how many pieces of the cloth you can touch. Can you touch the long pieces? Can you touch the short pieces too?"

HINTS:

1. Cord should be strung at such a height that the long strips of cloth may be touched easily. The short ones present more of a challenge.

2. Stress jumping straight up and not forward.

3. For variety, old clothes (old socks of different sizes, old shirts, old trousers, etc.) may be used in place of the cloth strips.

ACTIVITY: Wand Balance

EQUIPMENT: A wand for each child.

EXPLANATION:

1. Children should be spread out around room with plenty of space between them.

2. "Find the center or middle of your wand. Can you place the palm of your hand under the center of the wand and balance it? Try not to let it fall! Balance it the same way with your other hand."

DEVELOPMENTAL MOTOR ACTIVITIES

3. "Stand the wand on end in the palm of one hand. Can you balance it so that it stays straight? Try not to let it fall! You will have to move your hand to keep it balanced and straight. Now try the same thing with your other hand."

4. "Can you drop the wand on one end and catch it after one bounce? Be sure to keep your eyes on it."

5. "Stand the wand on one end on the floor. Can you let go of it, turn yourself around one time, and catch it before it falls?"

6. "Can you walk around the room balancing the center of the wand in the palm of your hand? can you walk around the room balancing the end of the wand in your palm?"

HINT:

1. Rubber grips may be placed on the ends of the wands for protection.

ACTIVITY: Hula Hoops

EQUIPMENT: One hula hoop for each child.

EXPLANATION:

1. Children should be spread out around room with plenty of space in between them.

2. "Can you roll the hoop with your hand and keep it from falling over? Move all around the room with your hoop. Can you roll it with your right hand? Can you roll it with your left hand? Can you roll your hoop, run after it, and catch it before it falls?"

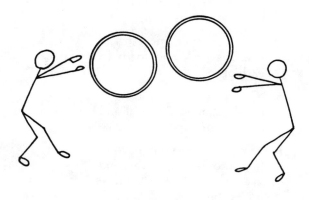

3. "Get a partner. Put one of the hoops down. Can you roll the hoop back and forth to each other? Keep your eyes on it, and try to catch it before it falls."

4. "Keep your partner. Each of you has a hula hoop. Can you roll the hoop back and forth to your partner while he rolls his hoop to you? Keep your eyes on both your partner's hoop and yours."

5. "Put your hula hoop on the floor. Can you walk around it? Can you walk in and out of your hula hoop? Can you walk with your right foot outside the hoop and your left foot inside the hoop? Can you jump into the hoop? Can you jump over the hoop?

6. "Get a partner. Put one hoop down. One partner holds the hoop. Can you walk through the hoop? How many ways can you find to move through the hoop? Pick up the other hoop? What can you do with two hoops?"

7. "Can you roll your hoop away so it will come back to you?"

ACTIVITY: Balloon Volley

EQUIPMENT: Inflated balloons with a penny inside each balloon.

EXPLANATION:

1. Children should be spread out, and each child should have a balloon.

2. "Can you throw your balloon into the air and catch it before it hits the ground?"

3. "Can you tap it lightly with both hands and keep it in the air? Keep tapping it to keep it up. Can you keep it up by tapping it with your right hand? Be sure to keep your eyes on the balloon. Can you keep it up by tapping it with your left hand? Alternate hands, tap it first with your right and then with your left. Keep your eyes on it."

4. "Get a partner and tap the balloons back and forth to each other."

5. "Can you tap your balloon lightly against the wall and keep it up?"

6. "Can you tap your balloon high into the air, turn around in a circle, and catch it before it hits the floor?"

7. "Toss the balloon into the air and see how many times you can clap your hands before you catch it."

8. "Tap the balloon into the air. Can you touch your knees and catch the balloon before it hits the floor? Can you slap your thighs and then catch it? Can you touch your toes and then catch it? Can you clap your hands behind your back and then catch it?"

HINTS:

1. As skill improves, many of these activities may be done with beanbags or rubber playground balls.

2. The children should be encouraged to keep their eyes on the object being caught.

⌒

ACTIVITY: Suspendible Ball

EQUIPMENT: Wiffle balls, string, and paddles.

EXPLANATION:

1. Suspend a wiffle ball from the ceiling using a length of string. Ball should hang about shoulder-high. There should be one ball for each child.

2. "Stand in front of your ball. Can you reach out and touch it with your fingers?"

3. "Can you hit it gently with your hands?"

4. "Pick up a paddle. Can you hit the ball with the paddle? Remember to hit it gently and to keep your eyes on it"

5. "Start the ball moving gently. Reach out and poke it using your finger. Try to poke it each time it swings back to you."

6. "Push the ball to make it move. Can you stop it with your hand? Remember to keep your eyes on the ball."

7. "Start the ball moving. Can you hit it with your hand? Hit it each time it swings back to you. Count the number of times you hit the ball. Watch the ball."

8. "Start the ball moving. Pick up a paddle. Can you hit the ball with the paddle? Hit it each time it swings back to you. Count the number of hits you get. Remember to keep your eyes on the ball."

ACTIVITY: Bounce, Throw, and Catch

EQUIPMENT: One playground ball for each child.

EXPLANATION:

1. Children should be spread out with plenty of space between them.

2. "Can you bounce the ball with one hand? Now try bouncing it with the other hand. Can you bounce it one time with your right hand and the next time with your left? Bounce the ball as low as you can. Bounce the ball as high as you can. Bounce the ball waist-high."

3. "Can you throw the ball up and catch it before it bounces? Can you throw the ball up, let it bounce once, and then catch it? Throw it up, let bounce two times, and catch it? Can you throw it up and catch it after the third bounce? Can you catch it after the fourth bounce? Count how many times you can toss the ball up and catch it without letting it bounce."

4. "Put one of the balls down. Get a partner. Can you bounce the ball to each other? Can you roll the ball to each other? Toss the ball gently in the air to each other. Move a little farther away from each other, and try bouncing the ball back and forth."

DEVELOPMENTAL MOTOR ACTIVITIES

5. "Can you walk around while you bounce or dribble the ball? Dribble the ball with your right hand. Now try dribbling it with your left hand. Can you run slowly and still dribble the ball?"

6. "Get a partner. Each has a ball. Can you bounce your ball to your partner while your partner bounces a ball to you? You must keep your eyes on your partner's ball as well as your own."

ACTIVITY: Bowling

EQUIPMENT: Old bowling pins or plastic bowling pins or plastic bottles, and balls.

EXPLANATION:

1. Pins may be set up in a variety of patterns.

2. "Can you roll your ball and knock over the pins in front of you? Can you count the number of pins you knock over?"

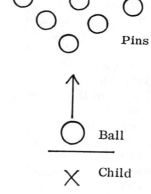

HINTS:

1. Start the children close to the pins so that every child is able to hit the pins successfully.

2. As skill improves, increase the distance between the child and the pins.

3. Points may be scored for each pin knocked over.

ACTIVITY: Target Rotation

EQUIPMENT: Boxes of various sizes open at one end, #10 size cans empty and clean, and small necked plastic bottles for targets. Yarn balls, rubber jar rings, and beanbags for throwing. One or two commercial or homemade games such as indoor shuffleboard and horseshoes.

EXPLANATION:

1. Five or more target game stations are set up around the play area. The children are divided into groups, and each group is assigned a game.

DEVELOPMENTAL GOALS AND ACTIVITIES

Groups rotate to different stations on signal.

2. Station set-up

Station #1: Three or four brightly painted boxes in a variety of sizes, open at one end, and yarn balls for throwing. "Can you toss your yarn ball and make it land inside one of the boxes? Can you make it land inside the largest box? Can you make it land inside the smallest box?"

Station #2: Four or five empty #10-size cans painted in bright colors and beanbags for throwing. "Can you throw your beanbag and make it land inside one of the cans? Can you make it land inside the closest can? Inside the can that is farthest away?"

Station #3: Indoor shorty shuffleboard game.

Station #4: Indoor horseshoe game (rubber horseshoes).

Station #5: Four or five small-necked plastic bottles for targets and rubber jar rings for throwing.

"Can you toss your rings and make them land over the neck of the bottles? Stand close to the bottles when you try this."

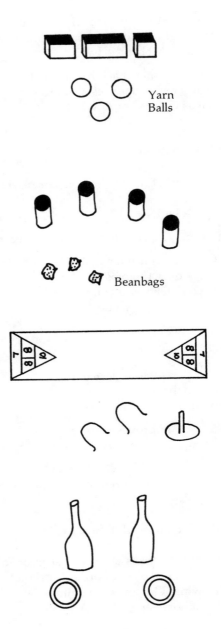

Yarn Balls

Beanbags

HINTS:

1. Target-toss games, either bought commercially or homemade, are innumerable. The teacher should use available equipment and a lot of imagination.

2. Start with the children about 5 feet away from the targets. Increase the distance as skill improves.

DEVELOPMENTAL MOTOR ACTIVITIES

ACTIVITY: Target Toss

EQUIPMENT: Large simple forms of animals, or clowns cut from heavy cardboard or plywood. Holes of various sizes are cut out for the eyes, mouth, nose, or in other places. The targets should be constructed with supports enabling them to stand alone, and can be painted in bright, attractive colors. Two to three beanbags for each child are needed.

EXPLANATION:

1. "Stand in front of one of the targets. Can you throw your beanbag and make it go through one of the holes in the target? Can you throw it through the big holes? Can you throw it through the little holes?"

HINTS:

1. Numbers may be painted by the large and small holes for scores. As skill improves, increases the distance between the target and the child.

2. Ask child to aim for a particular spot, such as the elephant's eye, the monkey's nose, or the clown's right ear.

3. Targets may be hung from the ceiling at different heights.

4. Stress good basic throwing skills.

ACTIVITY: Variety Toss

EQUIPMENT: Heavy cord with a variety of objects spaced and tied on it. This cord may then be tied between two standards or from one wall to another. Yarn balls, beanbags, or balls.

EXPLANATION:

1. Children stand about 6 feet away from the objects on the cord and try to hit them with yarn balls, beanbags, or rubber playground balls.

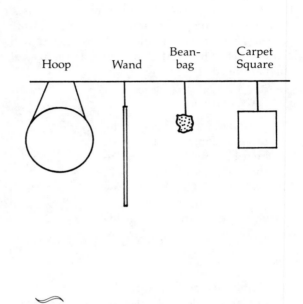

Hoop   Wand   Bean-bag   Carpet Square

HINTS:

- Stress good throwing skills such as use of opposite hand and foot, looking at the target, and follow through.
- As skill improves, have children back farther away before they throw at the targets.

2. "Count the number of objects you hit with your ball."

ACTIVITY: Games such as marbles, jacks, pick-up-sticks, checkers, Chinese checkers. Sewing with a dull-pointed needle and yarn on burlap. Other games or activities stressing eye-hand coordination.

EQUIPMENT: Games or activities listed above which have been bought commercially or homemade.

EXPLANATION:

1. The games may be set up in stations around the room or outdoor area.

2. A system of rotation may be used to assure that every child has an opportunity to play each game.

HINT:

1. These activities may be set up indoors or outdoors.

Coordination: Eye-Foot

ACTIVITY: Follow the Footprints

EQUIPMENT: Large paper footprints placed in a pattern on the floor.

EXPLANATION:

1. "These footprints belong to a big giant who came through here last night. Can you start here and walk in the giant's footprints?"

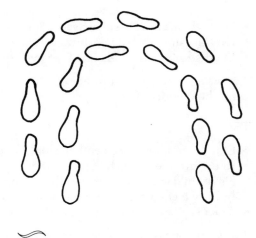

HINTS:

1. Different floor patterns may be used: geometric shapes, curved or straight paths.

2. Footprints may be marked "right" and "left."

ACTIVITY: Walk and Jump the Rope

EQUIPMENT: Jump ropes scattered on floor around room. One rope for each child.

EXPLANATION:

1. "Let's pretend your rope is a very narrow bridge. Can you walk all the way to the end without falling off? Remember to use your arms to help you balance."

HINTS:

- Have children walk heel to toe.
- Have children walk leading with right foot and sliding left up.
- Same as above, but lead with left and slide right.

2. "Now let us pretend that the rope is a tightrope in a circus. Can you walk the tightrope backwards?"

3. "The ropes are lying over an alligator pit now. See if you can walk sideways on the rope without falling in."

HINTS:

- Have children walk sideways leading with the right side.
- Do the same but lead with the left side.
- Do the same, but cross one foot over the other.

4. "Let us use our ropes for jumping now. Pick them up, and see if you can turn and jump them yourselves."

HINTS:

- One person holds each end of a long rope. Swing the rope back and forth close to the ground. The child jumps it as it swings.
- Have child stand in center with the rope on the outside. Swing it over child's head; the child should jump it as it touches the ground.
- Teacher may have to give verbal commands telling child when to jump.

5. "Put your rope on the floor. Can you jump over it without touching it?"

HINTS:

- Have children jump back and forth over their own ropes.
- Have children move around the room jumping over other ropes as they come to them.

ACTIVITY: Pathfinder

EQUIPMENT: Chalk or Tape.

EXPLANATION:

1. Curved, zig-zag, and straight paths are drawn or taped on the floor. Children are asked to move around the floor until they come to a path. The teacher gives verbal instructions as they move.

2. "Pretend you are an Indian walking through the woods. When you come to a path, see if you can walk forward on it without falling off. Walk forward on each path you find. Keep moving around the room looking for paths."

3. "Keep moving on the paths. Now see if you can walk backwards on the paths you find."

4. "Can you walk sideways without falling off?"

5. "Can you run on the paths?"

6. "See if you can skip on the paths."

7. "Show me if you can gallop on the paths."

8. "Can you slide on the paths?"

9. "See if you can move in a different way on each path. Can you change levels as you move?"

ACTIVITY: Walk the Challenge Course

EQUIPMENT: Hoops, tape, jump rope, balance beams, beanbags, wands, or other available equipment.

EXPLANATION:

1. Children move through, around, over, or on the objects.

HINTS:

1. Directions may be called out as children move through the course.

2. After skill improves, children may run through the course.

ACTIVITY: Hoop Walk

EQUIPMENT: Six to eight hoops.

EXPLANATION:

1. Hoops are placed in some pattern on the floor.

2. Children are in a line in front of the hoops. "Can you walk forward stepping into each hoop without touching it? Can you do the same thing walking backward? Can you walk sideways without touching them?

3. "Can you walk on the right side of the hoops, stepping with one foot inside the hoops and the other one outside? Walk back the same way on the other side of the hoops. Try not to touch them."

4. "Can you hop on one foot inside each hoop without touching it? Try the same thing on the other foot. Now try hopping on both feet."

HINT:

1. A variety of locomotor movements may be used in moving around or in-and-out of the hoops—skipping, running, sliding, galloping, leaping, jumping. Stress that the children move without touching the hoops.

ACTIVITY: Balloon Burst

EQUIPMENT: Two inflated balloons for each child and string.

EXPLANATION:

1. Two balloons are blown up and tied on the right and left ankles of each child. On a signal, the children try to burst each other's balloons with their feet. The winner is the last child with an unbroken balloon.

2. Spread children out within the established boundaries. "When the whistle blows, try to break everyone else's balloons by stepping on them, but try to keep yours from getting broken. Use only the feet, and be very careful not to push anyone. The last one with an unbroken balloon is the winner."

ACTIVITY: Balloon-Foot Volley

EQUIPMENT: A blown-up balloon with a penny inside for each child.

EXPLANATION:

1. "Lie down on your backs. Can you keep the balloon in the air using only your feet? How many times can you kick it before it touches the ground?"

HINTS:

1. This activity should be done indoors, as the slightest breeze makes it difficult to control the balloon.

2. Start out with giant balloons; as skill increases use smaller ones.

ACTIVITY: Hopscotch

EQUIPMENT: Hopscotch patterns painted or chalked on sidewalk or floor.

EXPLANATION:

1. Several different hopscotch patterns should be available to the children.

2. "Can you hop on one foot where there is one number or letter, and land on two feet where there are two numbers or letters side by side? Try not to touch the lines as you hop."

ACTIVITY: Toss the Beanbag

EQUIPMENT: One beanbag for each child.

EXPLANATION:

1. "See if you can push the beanbag across the floor using first one foot and then the other. Keep the beanbag close to your feet as you move."

2. "Place the beanbag between your ankles or feet; can you jump it to your hands?"

3. "Place the beanbag on top of one foot. Can you toss it into the air and catch it with your hands? Try tossing it with your other foot."

4. "Place the beanbag on the top of one foot; can you toss it into the air and make it land on top of your head?"

5. "Get with a partner. Put one of the beanbags down. Place the other one on top of your foot, and toss it up so that your partner can catch it. Now let your partner toss it to you. Take turns tossing the beanbag back and forth. Be sure to try tossing it both with your right and left foot."

ACTIVITY: Circle Kick

EQUIPMENT: One playground ball.

EXPLANATION:

1. Children stand in a circle and attempt to kick ball between the other children and out of the circle.

2. "When the whistle blows, try to kick the ball out of the circle. Keep the ball below shoulder-height when you kick. Those in the circle should try to block the ball with their bodies to keep it from going out."

HINTS:

1. This game may be played with the children sitting in a circle and attempting to keep the ball inside by using only their feet.

2. Children may sit in two lines facing each other with legs outstretched. The ball is rolled between the two lines. The children from one line attempt to kick the ball over the heads of the children in the other line. Only feet may be used.

ACTIVITY: Getting a Kick out of Sports

EQUIPMENT: Soccer balls or rubber playground balls—one for each child. Cones or plastic bottles for obstacles.

EXPLANATION:

1. "Can you move the ball all around the floor using only your feet? Be sure to keep the ball close to your feet at all times. Tap the ball first with one foot and then with the other."

2. "Find a partner. Using only one ball, can you pass the ball back and forth to each other using only the feet? See if you can stop the ball using only one foot."

3. Scatter the cones all around the floor. "Can you dribble the ball with your feet between and around the cones without touching them? Try to keep your ball under control at all times."

4. Take children to playground. "Put the ball on the ground in front of you. Now kick it as hard as you can. Run after the ball and kick it again."

5. Spread children out on playground. "Hold the ball with both hands in front of you. Drop it, and kick it before it hits the ground. This is called punting the ball. Can you punt the ball high into the air?"

6. "Drop the ball from both hands in front of you, let it bounce once, and then kick it. Remember to keep your eyes on the ball."

ACTIVITY: Foot Bowling

EQUIPMENT: Old bowling pins or plastic bottles, and playground balls.

EXPLANATION:

1. Pins are set up, and children kick the ball in an attempt to knock them over.

2. "Can you knock the pins over by kicking the ball at them? Count how many pins you knock over. Try kicking the ball with your other foot."

DEVELOPMENTAL GOALS AND ACTIVITIES

HINT:

1. Children should begin very close to the pins. As skill improves, increase the distance.

∿

ACTIVITY: Soccer Croquet

EQUIPMENT: Objects set up around room through which or around which the ball may be kicked (open-ended boxes, hoops set on end, chairs, benches, cones, etc.).

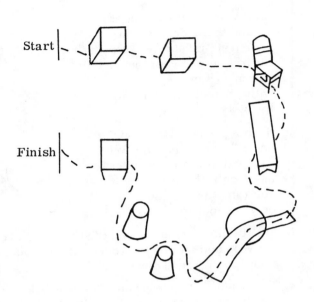

EXPLANATION:

1. Children must move the ball using only the feet under, around, or through various obstacles.

HINTS:

1. Encourage children to control the ball by kicking it gently through the course.

2. Encourage use of both right and left feet.

Coordination: Symmetrical

∿

ACTIVITY: Identification of Body Parts

EQUIPMENT: None.

EXPLANATION:

1. The children touch various body parts in response to the teacher.

2. "Touch your ears with your hands."

3. "Point to your mouth."

4. "Put your hands over your eyes."

5. "Put your finger on your chin."

6. "Point to your nose."

7. "Touch your legs with your hands."

8. "Put your hands on your arms."

9. "Point to your elbow."

10. "Pat your stomach."

11. "Put your hands up in the air."

12. "Touch your knees with your hands."

HINT:

1. Repeat the above, but ask children to respond with their eyes closed.

~

ACTIVITY: Movement of Body Parts

EQUIPMENT: None.

EXPLANATION:

1. The children move body parts in response to the teacher.

2. You may ask them to:
   - close their eyes
   - open their eyes
   - close their right eye
   - close their left eye
   - clap their hands
   - wiggle their fingers
   - bend at the elbows
   - bend at the knees
   - turn their heads
   - open their mouths
   - wink their eyes
   - squint their eyes
   - bend their necks
   - wiggle their toes
   - extend their arms
   - extend their hands
   - open their hands
   - wiggle their noses
   - shake their heads
   - nod their heads

~

ACTIVITY: Exploring Both Sides Through Movement

EQUIPMENT: None.

EXPLANATION:

1. The teacher presents a problem in the form of a question or statement, and the children respond with appropriate movements.

2. "See if you can make small forward circles with your left arm. Now try the same thing with your right arm. Can you do the same thing going backward? Try both arms together."

3. "How high can you kick your right leg in front of you. How high can you kick your left leg?" Repeat the same to the back.

4. "Can you move your right leg and right arm at the same time?" Repeat this with the left arm and leg, the right arm and left leg, and the left arm and right leg.

5. "Can you hop forward on your right foot while you make circles with your right arm?" Repeat the same with left foot and arm, right foot and left arm, and left foot and right arm.

6. "Lying on your back, can you move your right arm and leg at the same time?" Repeat with left arm and leg, right arm and left leg, and left arm and right leg.

7. "Lying on your back, can you touch your right foot with your right hand?" Repeat using left foot with left hand, right foot with left hand, and left foot with right hand.

HINT:

1. The variety of movements that may be presented to the children is almost limitless. With a little imagination and interest, teachers can provide hours of creative and stimulating experiences for their children with this activity.

ACTIVITY: Exploring Both Sides With Balloons

EQUIPMENT: Two inflated balloons for each child. The balloons should be weighted with a penny or small pebble.

EXPLANATION:

1. The children should be spread out with one balloon for each child.

2. "Can you keep the balloon in the air using only your right hand? Can you do this using your left hand?"

3. "Will the balloon stay up if you tap it first with one hand and then with the other?"

4. "Can you keep two balloons in the air at the same time?"

5. "Lying on your back, can you keep the balloon in the air using only your feet? Can you use your hands and feet together?"

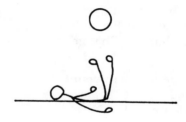

6. "Kneel on both knees. Can you keep the balloon up using only your left hand? Can you do this with your right hand?"

7. "Find a partner. Can you hit the balloon back and forth using only the right hand?" Have the children use the left hand, right foot, and left foot.

8. "Can you hop on your right foot and at the same time keep the balloon up with your hands? Try the same thing hopping on your left foot."

HINT:

1. Many other movement combinations utilizing hands and feet may be used.

ACTIVITY: Exploring Both Sides with Balls

EQUIPMENT: One playground ball for each child.

EXPLANATION:

1. The children should spread out with plenty of room between them. Each child is given a ball.

2. "See how high you can throw the ball with your right hand." Now use the left hand.

3. "Can you roll the ball to your partner using only the right hand?" Now use the left hand.

4. "See if you can keep your right hand on the ball and roll it all the way to the black line. Come back using your left hand."

5. "Toss the ball up with your right hand, and catch it with your left hand." Change hands.

6. "Bounce the ball with your right hand." Next, bounce with the left hand.

7. "Can you move and keep bouncing the ball with your right hand?" Now use the left hand.

8. "See how many different ways you can throw the ball to your partner using your right hand." Try throwing with the left hand.

9. "Put the ball on the floor. Kick it softly to your partner with your right foot." Next, kick with the left foot.

10. "Can you walk and keep moving the ball with your right foot first and then your left foot?"

11. "Can you drop the ball from your waist and kick it with your right foot?" Now use the left foot.

12. "Sit down facing your partner. See if you can roll the ball back and forth using only your right hand." Next, roll using the left hand.

13. Try other combinations as well.

HINTS:

1. When working on symmetrical activities, always counter a movement or action using the right hand or foot with a movement or action using the left hand or foot.

2. Many of the above activities may be done with yarn balls or beanbags.

~

ACTIVITY: Tug-of-War

EQUIPMENT: Tug-of-war ropes—long and short.

EXPLANATION:

1. Children should be paired according to size. Each pair is given a tug-of-war rope.

2. "Take hold of the end of your rope. Keep the rope straight, but do not begin to pull until the whistle blows. Bend your knees, and use your whole body to help you pull."

HINT:

- The center of the rope should be marked with a piece of tape. This tape is then lined up over a line on the floor. The winner is the one pulling his opponent over the line.

3. Use a long rope tied together at the ends. Place the rope on the floor in the shape of a circle. The children spread themselves around the circle, behind the rope. The rope is picked up and held taut, but no pulling begins until the signal is given.

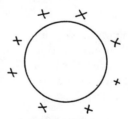

4. Variations with a single tug-of-war rope with loops on the end:
    - "Can you pull your partner over the line using only your right hand? Now try using only your left hand."
    - "Can you pull better with both hands?"

- "Sit down and hook the end of the rope over your right foot. On the signal, pull against your partner. Now try the same thing with your left foot."
- "Grasp the rope with your right hand and with your body supported on three parts. Can you still pull against your partner? Try the same thing with your left hand."
- "Stand back-to-back with your partner. Put the *loop* of the rope around one leg. Walk forward until the rope is taut. On the signal, pull against your partner."

ACTIVITY: Angels-in-the-Snow

EQUIPMENT: None.

EXPLANATION:

1. The children lie on their backs and move their arms and legs in response to the teacher. All movements should be done with the body parts in contact with the floor.

2. "Can you move your right arm up over your head? Bring it back to your side, and try moving your left arm in the same way."

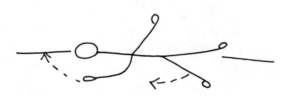

3. "How far can you move your right leg? Remember that your leg must touch the floor at all times. How far can you move your left leg?"

4. "Can you move your right arm and right leg together without raising them from the floor? Now try your left arm and leg?"

5. "Can you move your right arm and left leg at the same time? How about your left arm and right leg?"

6. "Can you move both arms and legs at the same time? Remember to keep them in contact with the floor."

HINT:

1. With young children the teacher may have to point to the body part or parts to be moved.

ACTIVITY: Imitation of Postures

EQUIPMENT: None.

EXPLANATION:

1. The children stand in front of the teacher and attempt to imitate arm and leg movements.

2. "Can you move your arms and legs exactly like me? Be sure you look exactly as I do."

3. The possibilities are limitless, but see the diagram for a few suggestions:

HINT:

1. After a little practice have the children get a partner with whom they will take turns imitating postures.

ACTIVITY: Magic Carpet Squares

EQUIPMENT: Carpet square on a smooth floor. One carpet square for each child.

EXPLANATION:

1. Spread carpet squares out around floor. The children go to a square and kneel on it.

2. "Can you slide yourself forward on your magic square using both hands together? Try the same thing going backward."

3. "Can you slide yourself forward using first one hand, then the other? Can you go backward the same way?"

4. "Lie on your stomach on your carpet square. Can you still slide yourself forward using both hands together? See if you can go backward the same way."

5. On stomach, "See how you would slide forward using first one hand, then the other. Now try it backward."

6. On stomach, "See how you would slide forward using both hands together, but pushing first with one foot and then with the other."

7. On stomach, "Can you slide forward using first your right hand and right foot together, then your left hand and foot."

8. On stomach, "Can you move sideways on your magic square?"

9. "Sit on your square. Can you move now? In how many different directions can you move?"

HINT:

1. Scooter boards may be used in place of carpet squares.

Space and Direction

Once children have developed an awareness of their bodies, they must be able to control their movements through space (their surroundings), and to change the direction of their movements when necessary.

Through your guided learning experiences, children should be given the opportunity to explore space through movement—backward, forward, sideways, right, left, and so on. This exploration can also include different levels, speeds, and patterns of movement. Such teacher guiding statements as "walk low to the ground, medium, high" (levels of space); "run quickly, slowly" (speeds); or "skip in a circle, a square" (patterns) can be created to help children explore space in meaningful ways.

Direction is another extremely important concept that children must master. This includes such directions as in front of, in back of, to the side, above, below, and so on.

Through many movement experiences involving space and direction, children will develop greater movement efficiency thus becoming more confident in their ability to manage their bodies in a variety of daily situations.

ACTIVITY: Concepts

EQUIPMENT: 1 table, 2 chairs, 1 mat, 1 long rope, 1 short rope, 1 door, chalk circle on floor.

EXPLANATION:

1. Equipment should be scattered around area. The chairs should be placed so that the child can walk between them.
2. "Can you point up?"
3. "Can you point down?"
4. "Raise your right hand."
5. "Can you climb over the table?"
6. "Crawl under the table."
7. "Can you stand in front of a chair?"
8. "Stand behind a chair."
9. "Sit in a chair."
10. "Find a circle. Can you jump into the circle?"
11. "Can you jump out of the circle?"
12. "Lie down on the mat."
13. "Stand off the mat."
14. "Pick up the long rope."
15. "Find the short rope, and pick it up."
16. "Can you place your feet above your head?"
17. "Place your hand below your knees."
18. "Find the circle. Can you walk around the circle?"
19. "Walk through the door."
20. "Can you walk between the chairs?"

ACTIVITY: Directional Course

EQUIPMENT: Chairs and wands

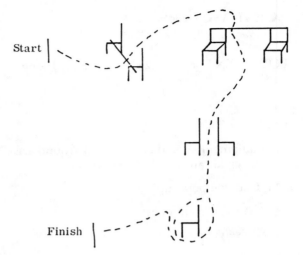

EXPLANATION:

1. Set up a directional course which will require the child to go over, under, between, and around certain obstacles.

2. "Can you step over the first wand? Can you go under the next wand? Can you walk between the chairs? Can you walk around the chair?"

HINT:

1. Other objects may be used for obstacles: tables, desks, cones, and wands.

⁓

ACTIVITY: Listen and Do

EQUIPMENT: None.

EXPLANATION:

1. Children should be spread out around entire area. Give simple instructions for children to follow:
   - "Can you walk forward?"
   - "Can you walk backward?"
   - "Show me how you walk sideways."
   - "Can you skip forward?"
   - "Can you slide sideways?"
   - "Can you skip backward?"
   - "Gallop forward."
   - "Hop forward."
   - "Can you hop backward?"
   - "Hop sideways to the right."
   - "Hop sideways to the left."
   - "Can you leap forward?"
   - "Jump forward."
   - "Jump backward."
   - "Jump to the side."

HINT:

1. Teacher may want to write some directions on flash cards and hold them up for the children to read.

ACTIVITY: Log Roll

EQUIPMENT: Flat mats or inclined mats.

EXPLANATION:

1. Have the children lie on their stomachs at one end of the mat with their hands over their heads.

2. "Can you roll like a log all the way to the end of the mat? Try to roll straight down the mat. Be sure to keep your eyes open."

HINT:

1. Spotters should be at the children's heads to prevent them from rolling onto the floor and hitting their heads.

ACTIVITY: Space Walk

EQUIPMENT: Sidewalk or other open area on which patterns may be painted.

EXPLANATION:

1. Directions may be painted beside each floor pattern, such as hop right and hop left. Children start at the beginning and follow the painted space walk.

HINTS:

1. The space walk may include anything the teacher deems necessary.

2. If directions are placed on movable cones instead of being painted on the sidewalk, the space walk may be changed periodically.

3. Children unable to read may be talked through the space walk by the teacher.

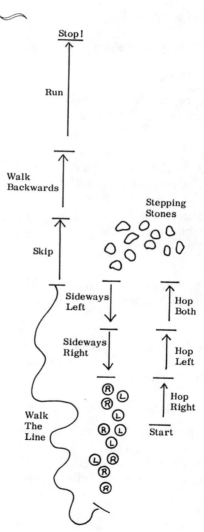

Body Image

A good body image is basic to the development of perceptual-motor skills. Through guided participation in physical activities, children can explore and discover how their bodies are capable of moving. "How high can you jump, stretch like a rubber band, or how big can you be?" are only three of the almost limitless number of questions to which you can ask your children to respond. Being able to identify their body parts and distinguish between the right and left sides of the body are also vitally important.

Individual achievement levels are inseparable from self-concept, how one feels about oneself. For the child, then, this becomes crucial. As the teacher you are in a unique position to help each one of your children discover their individual physical uniqueness in a positive and encouraging way.

ACTIVITY: Body Outline

EQUIPMENT: A large sheet of paper and crayons.

EXPLANATION:

1. Have the child lie on his back on a large sheet of paper. Use a crayon to outline his body.

2. Once the outline is completed, the child may be asked to add other body parts such as eyes, ears, nose, mouth, and fingers. Clothes may be colored in also.

HINT:

1. Older children may draw around each other.

ACTIVITY: Follow the Leader

EQUIPMENT: None.

EXPLANATION:

1. One child is the leader and is followed in a line by the other children. As they walk, the leader calls out a body part. The children must touch that body part while continuing to walk. The leader may call out: ears, neck, nose, shoulders, stomach, knees, ankles, elbows, head, back, legs, or arms.

DEVELOPMENTAL MOTOR ACTIVITIES

HINTS:

1. The leader should be changed frequently.

2. Arm positions and movements may be practiced in the same way: right arm up, left arm up, both arms up, both arms extended, or both arms swinging.

～～

ACTIVITY: Contacting Body Parts With Available Objects or Other Body Parts

EQUIPMENT: None.

EXPLANATION:

1. "Touch your knees to the floor."

2. "Touch your hands to the floor."

3. "Can you make your elbows touch your knees?"

4. "Can you touch your hand to your wrist?"

5. "Stand so that your arms are touching your sides."

6. "Can you make your nose touch the floor?"

7. "Touch your foot to your head."

8. "Stand so that your heels are touching the wall."

9. "Make your knee touch your chin."

10. "Hold your ankles with your hands."

11. "Can you kneel and put your ear on the seat of the chair?"

HINTS:

1. Use objects that are easily available.

2. Many other variations are possible.

～～

ACTIVITY: Simon Says

EQUIPMENT: None

EXPLANATION:

1. Play "Simon Says," but use the movements of specific body parts as commands. Simon says
   - bend your elbows.
   - snap your fingers.
   - close your eyes.

- open your mouth.
- shrug your shoulders.
- put your hands on your knees.
- stamp your feet.
- stand on tiptoes.
- clap your hands.
- point to your nose.

HINT:

1. Use a child to play the part of Simon. Change the leader frequently.

〜

ACTIVITY: Shadow Designs

EQUIPMENT: Opaque projector, movie projector, or other light source.

EXPLANATION:

1. Aim the light from the projector against a wall and have the child step in front of the light, creating shadows.

2. "Make your shadow as big as you can."

3. "Make it as small as you can."

4. "How tall can you make your shadow?"

5. "How short can you make it?"

6. "Can you make your shadow very wide?"

7. "Can you make it very narrow?"

8. "Pretend you are a bird. Can you make your shadow look like a bird?" Repeat this using other animals such as an elephant, a monkey, or a dog.

9. "How can you make your shadow move?"

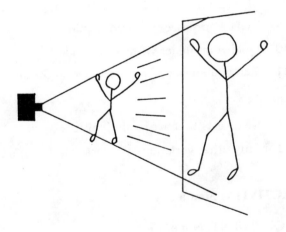

10. "Move only your fingers. How many different ways can you move them? Keep watching your shadow as you move them in many ways—Continue this, but move only arms, head, legs or feet.

11. "How many different ways can you make your arms bend? What part of your arm bends? (Elbow.) Can you make your arms bend at the elbow, then stretch them out again? Watch your shadow as you move—Now ask about the legs (bend at the knee), head (bend at the neck), feet (bend at the ankle), hands (bend at the wrist), and body (bends at the hips and/or waist).

12. "Can you make a design with your shadow? What else can you make your shadow do? Can it jump up? Can it hop? Can it walk? Can it run in place? Can it leap? Can it skip?"

13. "See what else your shadow can do."

ACTIVITY: Human Stick Figures

EQUIPMENT: None.

EXPLANATION:

1. Six children work together to make the shape (with their bodies) of a human stick figure lying on the floor.

2. At first, parts may be assigned: "Paul, you be the head; Mary, you be the right arm."

3. Once the body is made, the parts may move. "Mary, you are the right arm. Can you make it stretch? How else can you make the arm move?" Do the same with the other children.

4. You may ask the children to respond to commands such as: "Bend the right leg. Raise the right arm. Bend the left arm."

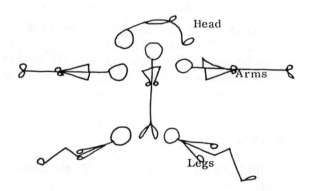

ACTIVITY: Body Jump

EQUIPMENT: Chalk or tape.

EXPLANATION:

1. A large stick figure of a person is drawn or taped on the floor for each child. The children are asked to hop or jump from one body part to another.

2. "Can you stand on the head and jump to the neck?"

3. "Can you jump from the neck to the right hand?"

4. "Jump from the right hand and see if you can land on the waist."

5. "Can you jump from the waist to the left hand?"

6. "Now try jumping from the left hand to the left foot."

7. "See if you can jump from the left foot to the right foot."

8. "Stand on the right foot. Can you walk up the right leg, jump to the head, and then walk backwards to the left foot?"

9. "Stand on the right hand. Can you hop on one foot to the left hand?" Many other variations are possible and should be used.

10. "Stand in front of your stick figure. I will call out the name of a body part, and you run and stand on it as fast as you can. When I blow the whistle, come back and stand in front of your stick figure, ready for the next call. Head!" Pause long enough to be sure that every child has responded correctly, then blow the whistle. Then, call "Leg!" and so on.

ACTIVITY: Create a Body

EQUIPMENT: A variety of available materials: beanbags, boxes, cans, hoops, balls, wands, ropes.

EXPLANATION:

1. Using the materials made available by the teacher, the children build a body on the floor.

DEVELOPMENTAL MOTOR ACTIVITIES

2. "Can you build a human body using the boxes, hoops, cans, beanbags, and other materials you see here?"

HINT:

- The older children may be given time to experiment on their own, but it may be necessary to guide the younger children by saying, "Look at all of this equipment. Can you see something that would make a good head? What comes after the head? Can you see something we could use for the neck?"

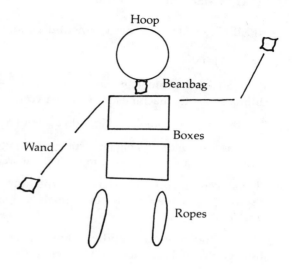

3. When the children have finished, ask them to study the body they created for several minutes. Afterward, take the different parts, stack them in a pile, and see how quickly they can put the body back together again. For added interest, let the children give their body a name (Fred, Sam, Hazel, etc.). "Let us take 'Sam' apart and stack him in a pile. When the whistle blows, see how fast you can put 'Sam' back together again."

4. Using old clothes and other available materials, help your children make a three-dimensional straw man to keep in the classroom.

Rhythm

Rhythm fulfills an inherent need in children of all ages. It serves as an exciting opportunity for creative self-expression through freedom of movement. Through rhythm, children can experience the joy and exhilaration of moving in time to the beat of a drum, the ring of a tambourine, or the tempo of a record.

Through fundamental rhythms, children learn to move effectively and efficiently by integrating different body parts into a smooth functioning whole. They develop feelings of grace and poise which serve to enhance feelings of self in relation to their capabilities.

Rhythm is an area of the curriculum in which all children can meet with success. It provides another opportunity for positive self-expression and growth in a most desirable manner.

ACTIVITY: Make-Believe World

EQUIPMENT: Suitable accompaniment depending on the individual situation.

EXPLANATION:

1. Individually or in small groups, children make-believe that they are other people, animals, plants, machines, or weather conditions.

2. "Pretend you are soldiers. How do soldiers march?"

3. "You are the pilot of a big jet airplane. Can you show me some of the things you would do? Can you take off in your plane? Can you land it?"

4. "Let's pretend you are monkeys in the jungle. Show me how monkeys move— Pretend the same with other animals like elephants, tigers, dogs, snakes, and ducks.

5. "A spell has been cast, and you have all been changed into witches! Show me how you would act. How do witches fly?"

6. "Now you are monsters from another world. How would you move?"

7. "Pretend you are a train. Can you go forward? Can you go backward? How does a train move going up a big steep mountain? How does it move coming down the mountain?"

8. "Have you ever ridden in a big truck? Pretend you are driving the truck. How would you move? Can you drive the truck on a winding mountain road? How does a truck sound?"

9. "Let's make-believe that you are the leaves on a big tree. How do the leaves move when the wind blows? What happens to leaves that have been blown down? Do they move when the wind blows? How do they move?"

10. "There is a terrible storm coming our way. First comes the wind. Can you move like the wind in a storm? Next comes the rain. What does rain look like? Then the lightning flashes in the sky. Now you are the lightning—Children may be divided into three groups and act out the storm together. One group acts out the wind, one the rain, and one the lightning.

∽

ACTIVITY: The Orchestra

EQUIPMENT: None.

EXPLANATION:

1. Small groups of children (four to five) choose an instrument to imitate. They may imitate it in terms of its shape, sound, and movement.

(Example: one group may choose a drum, another a violin, another a guitar.) Each group practices and then performs for the rest of the children who try to guess what instrument they were imitating.

HINTS:

1. You may want to provide each group with a picture of the instrument they chose and discuss some of its qualities—how it moves, what sound it makes.

2. Use a simple tune or song for all groups, such as Twinkle, Twinkle Little Star. Each instrument would then play the same tune.

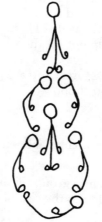

Bow—
Child moves over other children and makes sound of violin.

3. After the instruments have been presented to the group and identified, the entire class may perform the tune together making a symphony orchestra.

~

ACTIVITY: Dramatization of Creative Rhythms

EQUIPMENT: None.

EXPLANATION:

1. Individually or in small groups children dramatize
   - the interpretations of familiar stories or nursery rhymes such as The Three Bears, Little Red Riding Hood, The Three Little Pigs, or Mary Had A Little Lamb.
   - playing sports activities such as basketball, boating, tennis, golf, archery, football, swimming, track and field, or hockey.
   - making a snowman. "Pretend it is snowing; can you gather some snow and make a big snowman? What parts does a snowman have? Can you make those parts out of snow?"
   - flying a kite. "It is a very windy day, and you are flying a kite. How strong is the wind today? Show me. Hang on to your kite string; can you feel the kite pulling you?"

- climbing a mountain. "The mountain is steep, and you have to crawl up it very slowly. Can you make it to the top?"
- being in the woods. "Let us skip down this trail in the woods. Can you climb up on this tree branch and jump down? Here comes a big bear! Let's run!"
- building a house. "We need some big boards for our house. Can you pick up the boards and make the walls? Hammer the nails into the wood so the walls stay up. Let us all help put on the roof and nail it down. Can you paint the house?"
- shopping in a grocery store. "You are going shopping in a grocery store. Can you show me how you shop?"

HINTS:

1. Records may be used for accompaniment, or a tape may be recorded to fit the music to the dramatization.

2. The class may be divided into groups with each group practicing on its own, then presenting a dramatization to the rest of the class.

3. The children may want to construct simple props to aid in the presentation of the dramatization.

ACTIVITY: Move to the Drum (This activity should be used when presenting a particular beat [4/4, 6/8, etc.] to the children for the first time.)

EQUIPMENT: Drum.

EXPLANATION:

1. The teacher uses a basic beat on the drum and helps the children to understand it and feel it.

2. "Sit down and listen to the beat. Can you count the beat with me?"

3. "Let us clap hands to the beat of the drum."

4. "Clap your hands loudly on the accented beat and softly on the unaccented beats."

5. "Can you change the position of your arms on the accented beat and hold that same position on the unaccented beats?" Have children do the same with one arm, one foot, two feet, and so forth.

6. "Can you change the position of your arms on every beat? Can you change the position of your feet on every beat?"

Standing

7. "Can you stamp your foot to the beat of the drum? Stamp it loudly on the accented beat and softly on the unaccented beat."

8. "Move your arms in a different position on each beat." Do the same with legs.

9. "Can you move your body parts in unison (together) to the beat? Can you move first one body part and then another to the beat of the drum?"

10. "Make a body shape on the accented beat and hold it on the unaccented beats."

Moving

11. "Can you walk to the beat of the drum?"

12. "Walk to the beat of the drum, but bend your knees on every accented beat." Next, do the same, but touch floor on accented beat.

13. "Can you walk and clap your hands to the beat?"

14. "Move to the beat. As you move, change the position of your arms on every accented beat."

15. "The tempo is going to get faster, so now you must move faster. Listen to the beat as you move." Slow down the tempo, and do the same.

ACTIVITY: Band Member

EQUIPMENT: A variety of percussion instruments: drums, sticks, tambourines, cymbals.

EXPLANATION:

1. Divide the children into groups with four to five children in each group.

2. "Each person in each group choose an instrument you would like to play as you march with your group around the room."

HINTS:

1. At first, let the children beat out any rhythm they wish as they move around the room.

2. Assign a beat to each group: 2/4, 3/4, or 4/4.

3. Assign a band leader, and line the children up behind the leader as they march.

ACTIVITY: The Body With a Beat

EQUIPMENT: Drum or other percussion instrument.

EXPLANATION:

1. Select a beat, demonstrate and explain it to the children.

2. In response to the beat, ask the children to
   - "Put both hands on your: head head head head/ ears ears ears ears/nose nose nose nose/ toes toes toes toes." (Do the same with other combinations of body parts.)
   - "Put both hands on your: head/ears/nose/toes."
   - "Sit and put your head on your: arm arm arm arm/ leg leg leg leg/ knee knee knee knee/ foot foot foot foot." (Do the same with other body parts in different combinations.)
3. "I will now ask you questions about what your body parts do, and you can tell me." (Teacher asks, "Eyes eyes eyes eyes?" Children answer, "See see see see.") Repeat the question-answer sequence using: ears-hear, nose-smells, mouth-talks, feet-walk, and hands-touch.

HINT:

1. Use other beats or rhythms.

∿

ACTIVITY: Concepts With a Beat

EQUIPMENT: Drum or other percussion instrument.

EXPLANATION:

1. The teacher selects the beat to be used—in this case 4/4—explains it, and asks the children to respond by moving a part or parts of their bodies.
2. "Move your right arm: up up up up/down down down down." Repeat this with left arm, both arms, right and left legs, and combinations of arms and legs.
3. "Make your body: big big big big/small small small small."
4. "Stand so that you are: wide wide wide wide/narrow narrow narrow narrow."
5. "Reach with your arms; high high high high/low low low low."
6. "Move your arms: open open open open/closed closed closed closed." Do the same with legs.
7. "Walk: forward forward forward forward/backward backward backward backward."
8. "Make yourself: tall tall tall tall/short short short short."

HINTS:

1. For variety use another rhythm:
   - tall tall/short short
   - up up/down down
   - high high/low low

2. For more rapid movement try combining concepts:
   - tall short/tall short
   - up down/up down
   - wide narrow/wide narrow

~

ACTIVITY: Move to the Beats

EQUIPMENT: Various types of percussion instruments: drums, sticks, tambourines, others.

EXPLANATION:

1. Divide the children into groups with four to six children in each group.

2. Designate a leader who selects one of the instruments and then beats out a rhythm. The other children in the group respond by moving to the beat.

3. Try these variations:
   - Each child uses locomotor movements of own choice.
   - Each child uses nonlocomotor movements of own choice.
   - Entire group moves in unison.
   - Each moves with a partner.
   - Group plays follow-the-leader.
   - Teacher designates locomotor movements: walk, run, skip, and so on.
   - Teacher designates nonlocomotor movements: swinging, turning, swaying, bending, and so on.

HINT:

1. This activity should be used only after the children have gained some confidence in moving to basic beats or rhythms such as 2/4, 3/4, and 4/4.

~

ACTIVITY: Moving to Music

EQUIPMENT: Record player and various records. Any music may be used, but it should have an easily defined, definite beat. Children enjoy moving to modern music.

EXPLANATION:

1. In response to the rhythm of the music, have your children perform the following movements:
   - walk, run, skip, gallop, slide, hop, jump.
   - move their bodies in a high position while going left, right. (Use medium and low body positions and various directions while walking, hopping, running, etc.)

- clap their hands to the beat of the music.
- stamp their feet to the beat.
- swing their arms to the music (big and small movements).
- bend and stretch in time with the music.

HINT:

1. At first, children should be seated and listening while the teacher explains the rhythm or beat. Next, by clapping or moving an isolated body part, children should demonstrate that they hear and understand the beat or rhythm.

AQUATIC ACTIVITIES FOR ALL CHILDREN

Swimming is one of the most beneficial mediums of exercise. It provides an opportunity to improve such physiologic components as cardiovascular strength and endurance, and general muscular strength and endurance. Swimming exercises the entire body without putting extreme amounts of stress or tension on specific body parts. The body moves through a relaxing environment in which circulation, respiration, muscle endurance, and body secretions are elevated slightly to become more efficient and promote health-related fitness. Handicapped individuals do not necessarily have the opportunity to be totally active in all avenues of games and exercises, but swimming provides a medium from which most all handicapped individuals can gain physically and psychologically through exercise and participation.

The implementation of an adapted aquatics program must consider the objectives most suited for each individual. However, the most important considerations in developing an adapted aquatics program are (1) safety, (2) fun, and (3) learning. Without insuring that you have a *safe* and *enjoyable* environment, learning to swim will be very difficult for many nonswimmers. Ideas that help you establish a safe and fun learning environment include:

- Develop a trust relationship with the student.
- Build confidence through success.
- Be consistent in teaching techniques.
- Make safe, secure entries into the swimming pool.
- Eliminate excess equipment or toys on deck that may cause a person to stumble.
- Understand and be empathetic to the student's fear of the water.
- Have appropriate lesson plans developed prior to class.
- Provide positive reinforcement.
- Train volunteers prior to their taking an active role in the program.
- Teach towards independence.

Implications for Specific Disabilities in Aquatics

Regardless of the child's "normality" or "exceptionality," the most important consideration for an aquatics instructor is to evaluate what the student is *able* to do, not what they *cannot* do. In this section, we will highlight common potential problems for various disabilities. This is in no way either all inclusive or necessarily true for every student with the said disability. The teacher might consider these as assessment areas when evaluating the *abilities* of the student. According to Jeff McCubbin (1984, Boyd, McCubbin and Shasby, *Applied special physical education: A manual for the educator.* Burgess, 142-148), the following strategies are recommended when teaching aquatics to children with these common disabilities:

Cerebral Palsy
— abnormal muscle tone should be improved to facilitate better swim strokes
— warm water often aids in relaxation
— relaxation most often helps improve muscle tone
— often have difficulty floating due to hypertonicity
— do not encourage hyperextension of the neck in the back-lying (supine) position, as it may increase hypertonicity
— provide a calm environment by cutting down on splashing and extraneous noise
— head control, jaw closure, and breath control are often difficult
— bilateral strokes (finning, sculling, elementary backstroke, breaststroke) are more easily learned
— if the person is nonvocal, develop a communication system to use while in the water
— the most desirable teaching position is at the head of the swimmer, out of the way of the arm strokes
— realize that most kicks are difficult and decrease swimming stroke efficiency
— encourage *participation*, not *perfection*

Spinal Cord Injuries and Spinal Myelodysplasias (spina bifida)
— bowel and bladder incontinence may present concerns for the teacher and student
— swimming helps to prevent decubitis ulcers (pressure sores)
— encourage the use of socks if feet have a tendency to drag or scrape in shallow pools
— have a towel or mat available on the pool deck for transfers from the wheelchair to the deck
— be able to safely assist in transfers to the deck
— encourage independence around the pool
— help develop strength and endurance in the upper extremities
— high-level quadriplegics may have respiratory problems and may also need some assistance rolling from back to front
— may need assistance returning to the upright position while in the water

Muscular Dystrophies
— may have reluctance to get out of wheelchair and attempt swimming
— try not to overfatigue the swimmer
— avoid excessive chilling
— encourage breathing exercises
— encourage movement through full range of motion
— backstrokes often can be carried over for a longer period of time (i.e., finning, sculling, elementary backstroke, inverted breaststroke, backcrawl)
— transfer to the pool deck needs to be safe
— encourage independence in standing, walking, and swimming

Spinal Curvatures
— avoid repeated springboard diving
— help to strengthen antigravity muscles
— can improve general physical fitness
— if student wears an orthotic device, the device may be removed for swimming with no ill effects

Scoliosis
— students with scoliosis should work to improve trunk flexibility, strengthen postural muscles, and improve breathing muscles (diaphragm and intercostals)
— learn sidestroke, preferably with concave portion of primary curve down in the water to maximize stretch
— swim backcrawl to increase spinal flexibility
— bilateral strokes encourage muscle strengthening on both sides (particularly for Milwaukee brace wearers)

Kyphosis
— major objectives to stretch internal rotators and scapular abductors
— strengthen external rotators and scapular abductors
— specific strokes include inverted breast stroke, elementary backstroke, and backcrawl

Lordosis
— any swimming stroke to improve fitness is helpful
— kicking activities to stretch hip flexors and lumbar extensors (lower back)
— good practice may include placing a kickboard under the back (if laying on back) or stomach (if prone) to encourage keeping a flat back while kicking.

Mental Retardation
— make the instructions clear, concise, and consistent
— demonstrate frequently
— avoid unnecessary distractions like splashing, or games in other parts of the pool
— build in success
— tasks must be "overlearned" or practiced repeatedly
— incorporate games and game equipment to help teach academic skills (size, shape, color) and perceptual-motor skills (hand-eye coordination, body-awareness tasks)
— task analysis of swimming skills makes it easier to work on components of a skill
— may have problems coordinating arm strokes and kicks at same time
— limit the size of the teaching space

Amputee

Upper Extremity
— partial amputee should perform arm movements to the extent of the movement
— complete bilateral should concentrate on the kicking action for propulsion. The whip kick and scissors kick are most suitable
— complete unilateral, concentrate on sidestroke using a slightly deeper power stroke with the usable arm down

Lower Extremity
— use whatever kick is available that aids in propulsion
— bilateral above-knee amputee may have trouble with surface diving and recovery to the upright position

Visual Impairments
— get medical clearance
— should be given a tour of a new facility to identify pool structure and to become familiar with pool equipment and surroundings
— new situations may be very stressful to a blind individual, so do not rush through things
— many individuals, due to underdeveloped balance, may be "earthbound" and find it difficult to bring feet off the bottom
— minimize extraneous distractions and noise
— verbal cues must be clear, concise, and descriptive
— use tactile cues to reinforce verbal cues
— metronomes or auditory devices can be used to assist the blind swimmer in position orientation while in the pool

Seizure Disorders
— may actively participate in swimming
— lifeguard should be notified prior to the class
— it is *not* necessary to wear special hat or suit to identify the person
— diving from board or tower is usually inadvisable for safety reasons; however, diving from the deck is a suitable skill to develop
— build success to promote self-esteem

Chronic Obstructive Lung Disease
Asthma
— an outstanding form of exercise
— controlled respiration is a helpful skill to develop
— warm, damp environment is helpful for respiration

Cystic Fibrosis
— help promote social interaction
— force respirations good for lung expansion
— helps to unplug mucous secretions
— may help to inhibit kyphosis
— should avoid deep water diving if polyps are evident

Juvenile Rheumatoid Arthritis
— choose strokes dependent on active movement while in the water
— warm water helps to increase range of motion
— stressful situations for the joints should be avoided
— contact medical team to help identify specific aquatic exercises

Contraindications for Swimming

In developing an adapted aquatics program, the supervisor must be aware of certain conditions that make swimming inadvisable. A medical consultant should be available if questions arise. When no such consultant is available and a medical question remains unanswered, abstention from the activity is recommended. Medical approval should be indicated prior to the beginning of the program; however, a general contraindication list for swimming includes

- infectious diseases in the active stage (i.e., the person still has an elevated temperature),
- chronic ear infections,
- chronic sinusitis,
- allergies to chlorine or water,
- skin conditions such as eczema,
- open wounds and sores such as draining decubitus ulcers,
- osteomyelitis in the active stage,
- acute episodes of rheumatoid arthritis,
- venereal diseases, and
- severe cardiac conditions.

Lifts and Transfers

The most important aspect of transferring a person into the pool is insuring the safety of all who are involved. All too often, inappropriate techniques are used that frighten the swimmers and put them at a risk of unnecessary injury. The following steps are helpful:

- Think safety first! Employ all possible help when lifting a person. Depending on the person's size, two adults are usually adequate.
- Make certain that the brakes on the wheelchair are locked. If additional people are available, have someone hold the wheelchair in addition to locking the brakes.
- Use good body mechanics when lifting. The distance the person is lifted should be as small as possible.
- Lift the person in unison, with one person giving directions.
- Explain to the person prior to lifting him the plans of the lift to the deck, or have the person explain how he or she feels most comfortable being lifted.
- Lift the swimmer from the chair to the deck, then from the deck to the pool. The deck should be nonabrasive. If the deck is abrasive, use a towel or blanket to pad the surface.
- Insure that a helper is available to support the person on the deck if necessary.
- Always have a helper in the pool to help the swimmer into the water.
- If the swimmer is independent in transferring to the deck of the pool safely, provide a safe environment and promote the swimmer's independence, but be available to assist when necessary.

- Use ramps to transport the person into the water in a wheelchair when a lifting procedure is not possible.

Games and Game Equipment

The great thing about aquatics and equipment for the pool is that almost everything can be used. Leftover and inexpensive equipment often works best in a pool, provided that a little imagination goes along with it. Objects that sink can be used for retrieval games; floating objects have many uses.

Equipment that helps the beginning swimmer adjust to the water include sponges, wash cloths, squeeze water bottles, pots, pans, old milk jugs, blow tubes, straws, plastic buckets, and the child's favorite plastic game or toy.

Equipment that can be incorporated into games is unlimited. Examples include plastic balls, wiffle balls, balloons, deck tennis rings, hula hoops, kickboards, cones, nerf balls, golf balls, plastic flowers, basketballs, and beach balls.

Perceptual-motor skills and academic skills can be improved with equipment that incorporates shapes, textures, color, and sounds. Such equipment may include multicolored hats, sponges in shapes or numbered, squeeze toys, hoops, rings, and ropes. Ropes can be used to make many shapes and sizes. They can be used to develop concepts such as under, over, around, and through with consistent changes to help the child be more perceptive.

The imagination of the instructor determines the types of games that can be adapted for the water. Relays, tag games, and search and recover games are often used in the pool. New games designed for cooperation, as opposed to competition, can really improve the social interaction in the pool and make the games fun for all.

Summary

Aquatic programs for the handicapped offer tremendous benefits that may not be achieved through any other single medium. Physiologic, sociologic, and psychologic factors can all be improved through active participation in a recreational sport such as swimming. Swimming offers the opportunity for a handicapped individual to be able to move totally independent of all assistive devices such as wheelchairs, crutches, braces, and canes. Buoyancy helps promote active self-propulsion for those with otherwise limited movement potential. Swimming is not only a beneficial exercise for the handicapped, but more importantly, it provides a lifetime recreational and leisure-time activity.

GENERAL GUIDELINES FOR ADAPTING ACTIVITIES FOR ALL CHILDREN

The following information consists of methods of adapting or modifying games and activities to permit exceptional children to safely participate with their normal peers in typical elementary motor experiences. The material is rather generalized to ensure its maximum application.

General Considerations

1. Most children with permanent disabilities will have already developed necessary modifications to permit their participation in certain activities. Allow these children to proceed at their own rate of involvement. If they experience difficulty or cannot make the necessary adjustments, step in and assist.

2. Adaptations should be made to suit the child's abilities rather than his or her disabilities.

3. Modification of game rules should not be discouraged and should be regulated to meet the needs of the group.

4. Try not to change a game to such a degree that the children lose sight of what they started to play.

5. When working with a new student, begin by slowly and gradually introducing him or her to new activities. Keep in mind that the child may have some fear of new experiences, may become embarrassed, or may display a lack of initiative.

Methods of Modifying Games and Activities

1. Reduce the size of the playing area.
   a. Change the boundary lines.
   b. Increase the number of players.
   c. Decrease the height of the net or goal.
   d. Use equipment that will reduce the range of play.
   e. Remember net-type games may be played through a hoop.

2. Use lighter equipment:
   a. plastic bats, wiffle-type balls;
   b. large plastic beachballs, bladder balls; or
   c. yarn balls, styrofoam balls.

3. Slow down moving objects.
   a. Change the throwing style to underhand.
   b. Throw ball with one bounce.
   c. Roll the ball.
   d. Use a stationary ball. (Place it on home plate, or place it on a batting T.)
   e. Increase the size of the ball.
   f. Decrease the weight of the ball.
   g. Decrease the air pressure within the ball.

4. Modify the rules.
   a. Sit down or lie down rather than stand.
   b. Walk rather than run.
   c. Kick rather than strike.
   d. Throw or strike rather than kick.
   e. Permit additional trials—strikes, throws, or jumps.
   f. Allow for substitution.
   g. Reduce the time periods of the game.
   h. Reduce the number of points required to win a contest.

5. Provide additional rest periods.
   a. Discuss rule infractions.
   b. Discuss strategy and team play.
   c. Rotate players in and out of the game or into active and inactive positions.
   d. Reduce the time periods of the game.
   e. Provide quiet-type games which may keep the student busy during rest periods, such as nerf hockey, box soccer, darts, or ring toss.

Appendixes

Appendix A: Teaching Materials

A rather wide selection of books, films, filmstrips, records, and other teaching aids, including ideas on homemade equipment, is presented in this section. Most apply directly to perceptual-motor learning; however, other references from related fields such as motor learning and special physical education have been included when the authors felt that these sources offered useful material.

BOOKS

AAHPERD. (1972). *Annotated bibliography on perceptual-motor development*. Washington, DC: AAHPERD.

AAHPERD. (1976). *Motor fitness testing manual for the moderately mentally retarded*. Washington, DC: AAHPERD.

AAHPERD. (1976). *Physical education, recreation, and related programs for autistic and emotionally disturbed children*. Washington, DC: AAHPERD.

AAHPERD. (1978). *Testing for impaired, disabled, and handicapped individuals*. Washington, DC: AAHPERD.

Adams, R.C., & McCubbin, J.A. (1990). *Games, sports, and exercises for the physically disabled* (4th ed.). Philadelphia: Lea & Febiger.

Albinson, J.G., & Andrew, G.M. (Eds.). (1976). *Child in sport and physical activity*. Baltimore: University Park Press.

American Red Cross. (1977). *Adapted aquatics*. Garden City, NJ: Doubleday.

Arnheim, P.O., & Sinclair, W.A. (1979). *The clumsy child: A program of motor therapy* (2nd Ed.). St. Louis: C.V. Mosby.

Auxter, D., & Pyfer, P. (1989). *Principles and methods of adapted physical education recreation* (6th Ed.). St. Louis, MO: Times/Mirror Mosby.

Ayres, A.J. (1978). *Sensory integration and learning disorders*. Los Angeles: Western Psychological Services.

Barsch, R.H. (1968). *Achieving perceptual-motor efficiency*. Seattle, WA: Special Child Publication.

Benton, A.L. (1968). Right-left discrimination. *Pediatric Clinics of North America, 15,* 747-758.

Berry, K.E. (1967). *Developmental test of visual-motor integration*. Chicago: Follett Educational.

Bleck, E.E., & Nagel, D.A. (1987). *Physically handicapped children: A medical atlas for teachers* (2nd Ed.). New York: Grune & Stratton.

Boyd, C.E., McCubbin, J.A., & Shasby, G.B. (1984). *Applied special physical education: A manual for the educator.* Edwina, MN: Burgess.

Bruiniks-Oseretsky test of motor proficiency. (1978). Circle Pines, MN: American Guidance Service.

Cherry, C. (1968). *Creative movement for the developing child.* Belmont, CA: Fearson.

Connolly, K.J. (1970). *Mechanisms of motor skill development.* New York: Academic Press.

Corbin, C.B. (1973). *A textbook of motor development.* Dubuque, IA: Brown.

Cratty, B.J. (1969). *Motor activity and the education of retardates.* Philadelphia: Lea & Febiger.

Cratty, B.J. (1970). *Perceptual and motor development in infants and children.* Los Angeles: Macmillan.

Cratty, B.J. (1975). *Remedial motor activity for children.* Philadelphia: Lea & Febiger.

Cratty, B.J. (1989). *Adapted physical education for the physically handicapped* (2nd Ed.). Denver: Love Publishing.

Fairfax County Public Schools. (1978). *Project Beacon: Perceptual-motor activities handbook.* County School Board of Fairfax, VA.

Fait, H.F., & Dunn, J.M. (1984). *Special physical education: Adapted, corrective, developmental* (5th Ed.). Philadelphia: Saunders.

Fredericks, H.D., Baldwin, V.L., Doughty, P., & Walter, L.J. (1972). *The teaching research motor development scale for moderately and severely retarded children.* Springfield, IL: Charles C. Thomas.

French, R.W., & Jansma, P. (1982). *Special physical education.* Columbus, OH: Merrill.

Frostig, M., & Masslow, P. (1969). *Move-Grow-Learn.* Chicago: Follett Educational.

Frostig, M., & Masslow, P. (1970). *Movement education: Theory and practice.* Chicago: Follett Educational.

Gallahue, D.L. (1975). *Developmental play equipment.* New York: Wiley.

Geddes, D. (1974). *Physical activities for individuals with handicapping conditions.* St. Louis: C.V. Mosby.

Gilbert, A.G. (1977). *Teaching the three R's through movement experiences.* Edwina, MN: Burgess.

Godfrey, B.B., & Kephart, N.C. (1969). *Movement patterns and motor education.* New York: Appleton-Century-Crofts.

Horvat, M. (1990). *Physical education and sports for exceptional students.* Dubuque, IA: Brown.

Hotnour, M. (1990). *Physical fitness games and activities kit.* Englewood Cliffs, NJ: Prentice-Hall.

Johnson, & Lorderee (1976). *Motor fitness testing manual for the moderately mentally retarded.* Washington, DC: AAHPERD.

Kalakian, C.B., & Eichstaedt, L.H. (1987). *Developmental/adapted physical education* (2nd Ed.). Edwina, MN: Burgess.

Kephart, N.C. (1966). *The slow learner in the classroom.* Columbus, OH: Merrill.

Kidd, A.H., & Nivoire, J.L. (Eds.) (1966). *Perceptual development in children.* Madison, CT: International Universities Press.

Lerch, H.A., Becker, J.E., Ward, B.M., & Nelson, J.A. (1985). *Perceptual-motor learning— Theory and practice.* Palo Alto, CA: Peek Publications.

Levy, J. (1978). *Play behavior.* New York: Wiley.

McDaniel, J. (1976). *Physical disability and human behavior.* New York: Pergamon.

McGraw, M.B. (1966). *The neuromuscular maturation of the human infant.* New York: Hafner Press.

Montgomery, P., & Richter, E. (1978). *Sensorimotor integration for developmentally disabled children: A handbook.* Los Angeles: Western Psychological Services.

Moran, J., & Kalakian, L. (1977). *Movement experiences for the mentally retarded or emotionally disturbed child.* Edwina, MN: Burgess.

Morris, P.R., & Whiting, H.T. (1971). *Motor impairment and compensatory education.* Philadelphia: Lea & Febiger.

Mosston, M. (1965). *Developmental movement.* Columbus, OH: Merrill.

Orlick, T., & Botterill, C. (1975). *Every kid can win.* Chicago: Nelson Hall.

Radler, D.H., & Kephart, N.C. (1960). *Success through play.* New York: Harper & Row.

Seaman, J., & Depauw, K. (1989). *The new adapted physical education* (2nd Ed.). Mountain View, CA: Mayfield.

Shears, L., & Bower, E. (1974). *Games in education and development.* Springfield, IL: Charles C. Thomas.

Sherrill, C. (1986). *Adapted physical education and recreation: A multidisciplinary approach* (3rd Ed.). Dubuque, IA: Brown.

Werder, J.K., & Kalakian, L.H. (1985). *Assessment in adapted physical education.* Edwina, MN: Burgess.

Wessel, J., & Kelly, L. (1986). *Achievement based curriculum development in physical education.* Philadelphia: Lea & Febiger.

Wheeler, N.H., & Hooley, A. (1976). *Physical education for the handicapped.* Philadelphia: Lea & Febiger.

Wickstrom, R.L. (1977). *Fundamental motor patterns.* Philadelphia: Lea & Febiger.

Winnick, J. (1979). *Early movement experiences and development.* Philadelphia: Saunders.

Wiseman, D.C. (1982). *A practical approach to adapted physical education.* Reading, MA: Addison-Wesley.

AUDIOVISUALS

Films

Blocks . . . A Medium for Perceptual Learnings is a 16mm, 17-minute sound and color film that focuses on the perceptual learnings that are inherent in block building, derived from how children perceive the blocks with which they work and the space in which they build. The perceptual learnings are further detailed in relation to academic learnings. Campus Film Distributors Corporation, 20 E. 46th Street, New York, NY 10017.

Bridges to Learning is a 16mm, 30-minute sound and color film that depicts a kindergarten through sixth grade physical education program. Perceptual-motor activities are emphasized. Palmer Films, Inc., 611 Howard Street, San Francisco, CA.

Creative Body Movements is a 16mm, 11-minute color and sound film that shows primary children involved in perceptual-motor activities. Martin Moyer Productions, 900 Federal Ave. East, Seattle, WA 98102.

Discovering Rhythm is a 16mm, 11-minute sound and color film that depicts rhythm as an outgrowth of activities such as walking and running. Basic concepts related to rhythm are discussed. Universal Education and Visual Arts, 221 Park Avenue South, New York, NY 10003.

Movement Exploration is a 16mm, 20-minute sound and color film that shows activities for kindergarten through sixth grade children. The wide range of movement activities involves the child in the problem-solving approach. Documentary Films, 3217 Trout Gulch Rd., Aptos, CA 95003.

Movement Education: What Am I? is a 16mm, 11-minute color and sound film that shows children how to use their bodies to move in various ways. Film Associations, 11559 Santa Monica Blvd., Los Angeles, CA 90025.

Moveginic Curriculum is a 16mm, 30-minute black and white film that depicts a perceptual-motor activity curriculum for the educationally disadvantaged child. University of Wisconsin Bureau of Audio-Visual Instruction, University Extension, 1312 West Johnson, Madison, WI 53701.

Moving is Learning is a 16mm, 18-minute color and sound film that shows perceptual-motor retraining techniques used by a visual learning center to assist perceptually handicapped children. Canadian Association for Children with Learning Disabilities, Suite 322, 88 Eglinton Ave., East Toronto 315, Ontario.

Outdoor Play . . . A Motivating Force for Learning is a 16mm, 17-minute film with sound and color. This film presents the unique physical and intellectual development provided by outdoor play activities and the extensive use of improvised materials. Children interact with various materials and with each other in exploration of space, experimentation with balance, development of muscular coordination and body awareness. Developmental differences are related and self-determined activities and goals are shown. Campus Film Distributors Corp., 20 E. 46th St., New York, NY 10017.

Perc! Pop! Sprinkle! is a 16mm, 11-minute color and sound film that gives visual experiences for children to observe and then to express through movement. Martin Moyer Productions, 900 Federal Ave. East, Seattle, WA 98102.

Piaget's Developmental Theory I—Conservation (#7121) is a 28-minute color film that demonstrates the stages of the development of thinking in children and how to assess these with Piaget's theories. Children, ages 5-12, are presented tasks involving conservation of quantity, length, area, and volume. The characteristics of thought from pre-operational to form are identified. University of California Extension Media Center, Berkeley, CA 94720.

Piaget's Developmental Theory II—Classification (#7120) is a 17-minute color film that shows children at several developmental stages responding to tasks of differing mental operations essential to classification. University of California Extension Media Center, Berkeley, CA 94720.

Piaget's Developmental Theory IV—Growth of Intelligence in the Preschool Years (#7327) is a 30-minute color film which examines growth of thinking processes in the preschool years. Children, ages 3-6, are presented with tasks that reveal how they think as they sort objects, place them in one to one correspondence, or arrange them according to size. University of California Extension Media Center, Berkeley, CA 94720.

Readiness for Reading is a 16mm color and sound film that explains the desirability and necessity of five areas of reading readiness: perceptual, experiential, language, interest, and social-emotional. The teacher is shown ways to develop each area.

Educational Motion Pictures, Indiana University, Audio-Visual Center, Blooming-ton, IN 47401.

The Mountain Does It For Me, 16mm, 12-minute film, #F-143, and *Two, Three Fasten Your Ski*, 16mm, 17½ minute film #F-144 are two excellent films by Crystal Productions, Box 11840, Aspen, CO 81611, demonstrating the methods for teaching disabled children to ski. Featuring Hal O'Leary, one of the founders of skiing for the disabled. Medical aspects are discussed. Disabilities featured are cerebral palsy, amputations, spinal myelodysplasias, poliomyelitis, mental and sensory deficits, more.

Thinking, Moving, Learning is a 16mm, 20-minute color and sound film that depicts perceptual-motor activities for kindergarten and primary grade children. Bradley Wright Films, 390 N. Duane, San Gabriel, CA 91775.

Why Physical Education is a 16mm, 14-minute sound and color film that depicts the importance of physical education in developing hand, foot, and eye coordination which helps the mind and body to work together more effectively. The value of physical education in developing strength, flexibility, and endurance is identified. Audio-Visual Center, Indiana University, Bloomington, IN 47401.

Filmstrips

Approaches to Learning suggests practical classroom techniques for developing in young children the basic perceptual-motor, and cognitive skills that are prerequisite to academic success. This series provides a general background and understanding of the basic skills areas and their relationship to academic learning. Three film-strips with records or cassettes are available from Teaching Resources, 100 Boylston Street, Boston, MA 02116.

Developing Cognitive Skills in Young Learners is a series of filmstrips designed to help the child in the development of fundamental intellectual concepts such as ordering, grouping, and inferring. The child is helped in acquiring many of the perceptual and cognitive skills necessary for intellectual growth. Seven color filmstrips and guide from Educational Activities, Inc., Freeport, L.I., NY 11520.

54 Functional Words uses a multisensory approach—visual, kinesthetic and tactile—in teaching the functional words and signs of everyday life to primary classes. This series includes 9 color filmstrips, 54 flashcards, 64 page workbook and teacher guide from Warren Schloat Productions, Pleasantville, NY 10570.

Making Logical Judgements is a series of filmstrips designed to help the child develop fundamental intellectual concepts that are crucial to school learning. Experiences are offered to train the child in multiple categorization, relational concepts, visual comprehension, ability to recognize logical inconsistencies, and logical analysis. Seven color filmstrips and guide from Educational Activities, Inc., Freeport, L.I., NY 11520.

Perceptual Skills is a series of six filmstrips. Basic visual perceptions: color, form, size; perception of sound; perception of spatial relationships; figure ground discrimination; perception of parts to whole relationships; and perception of sequence. Activities of matching, recognizing, sorting and relative size, as well as activities to develop the concept of constancy are presented. Six filmstrips with records or cassettes from Teaching Resources, 100 Boylston Street, Boston, MA 02116.

Phrase Training Filmstrips Grade K-6 are a series of filmstrips designed to teach children to see phrases accurately and read from left to right. The child is helped to correct poor reading habits. Twelve filmstrips and guide from Educational Activities, Inc. Freeport, L.I., NY 11520.

Progressive Visual Perceptual Training Filmstrips Level I by Katherine H. O'Connor is a series of five filmstrips developed to help the student raise his visual perceptual skills. Look-alike words and word reversals are presented. Children are asked to see, recall, and physically reproduce what they saw. Five filmstrips and manual from Educational Activities, Freeport, L.I, NY 11520.

Sensory Awareness is a series of color-sound filmstrips to enrich sensory perception. They are designed to help children use their visual, auditory, and tactile senses more effectively in their gathering of information on the world around them. Four filmstrips with records or cassettes from Teaching Resources, 100 Boylston Street, Boston, MA 02116.

The Art of Seeing is a series of six color sound film strips which introduces the student to the language of visual perception and expression. It stimulates the student to make his or her own discoveries about painting, sculpture, architecture, and other media. Six filmstrips with teacher guide and records or cassettes from Warren Schloat Productions, Pleasantville, NY 10570.

Visual Discrimination Training Filmstrips is a series of filmstrips designed to develop speed and accuracy in recognizing likeness and differences in pictures from letters, numbers, words, phrases, and sentences. Ten filmstrips and manual from Educational Activities, Inc., Freeport, L.I., NY 11520.

Visual Perception Skills is a series of filmstrips designed to aid in the development of basic visual skills. Visual perception is promoted through activities involving visual memory, visual motor coordination, visual constancy, visual discrimination, visualization, figure-ground perception, and visual matching. Seven color filmstrips and guide from Educational Activities, Inc., Freeport, L.I., NY 11520.

Records

Creative Movement and Rhythmic Exploration (AR 533) by Hap Palmer. Exciting songs provide action and challenges for the child in creative movement, mimetics, and physical activity. Ways to move, geometric shapes, concepts, and sounds are explored.[1]

Developing Perceptual Motor Needs of Primary Level Children (AR 606-7). This record provides a training program to help pupils establish necessary perceptual-motor skills in agility, balance, combination balance and locomotor agility, turning, and complex locomotor agility.[1]

Discovery Through Movement Exploration (AR 534) by Layne C. Hackett. Children are challenged to seek motor solutions to problems in space-awareness classroom-related activities, ball and rope handling.[1]

Dynamic Balancing Activities (AR 657) This album is useful for training the child in both static and moving balance activities. These activities combined with various tasks should heighten the child's awareness of his or her body image.[1]

Dynamic Balancing Activities: Balance Beam Activities (AR 658). The activities in this album correlate balance and body image activities. The activities range from simple walking in various positions on the beam to more complex balance activities.[1]

Homemade Band (AR 545) by Hap Palmer. Directions are provided for making home instruments so the child can perform as a member of a band. The suggested activities should help the child in the development of body awareness, gross and fine motor coordination, auditory discrimination, rhythm, and freedom of movement.[1]

Getting to Know Myself (AR 543) by Hap Palmer. This "introduction to learning" covers such areas as awareness of body image and the body's position in space; identification of body places; objects in relation to body planes, body-part identification; movements of body; laterality of body; and feelings and moods.[1]

Learning Basic Skills Through Music, Volume I (AR 514) by Hap Palmer. Numbers, colors, the alphabet, and body awareness are presented in a happy rhythmic teaching program which is appropriate for preschool slow learners and early primary children. The record is also available in Spanish.[1]

Learning Basic Skills Through Music: Vocabulary (AR 521) by Hap Palmer. Through active participation, the child learns safety vocabulary, kinds of foods, parts of the body, and forms of transportation.[1]

Learning Basic Skills Through Music, Volume II (AR 522) by Hap Palmer. Games, songs teaching 11 colors, numbers to 20, subtraction, and telling time are included. There are also two reading-readiness games songs. This record is also available in Spanish.[1]

Match Readiness: Vocabulary and Concepts (AR 540) by Hap Palmer. Concepts such as big, little, long, short, shorter, same, like, different, before, after, in between, greater, and less are explored to help the child in math readiness.[1]

Music for Movement Exploration (KEA 5090) by Karol Lee. Unique musical effects bring out the original in each child.[1]

Relaxation—Impulse Control Through Relaxation (AR 655). This record introduces muscle activities to decrease levels of stimulation and increase muscular control. Children are helped to relax, to go slow, and to think.[1]

Simple Agility Movements for Impulse Control (AR 656). This album provides instructions for relaxation training as well as activities to aid children in controlling tension in specific parts of their body rather than permitting a spillover of tensions into all body parts when movement in only one part is desired.[1]

Sensorimotor Training in the Classroom (AR 532) by Linda Williams and Donna Wemple. Songs, cheers, folk music, chants, popular music, and poems are used with selected perceptual activities to develop body image, laterality, space directionality, basic movement, physical fitness, ocular training, and auditory discrimination.[1]

The Development of Body Awareness and Position in Space (AR 605). This record provides a researched training program to aid the student in awareness of his body and position in space.[1]

To Move Is To Be (KEA 8060) by Jo Ann Scher. Some twenty rock to classical musical selections guide the child into doing his or her own version of moving, bending, twisting, stretching, hopping, walking, and running.[1]

---

[1]The records may be ordered from Educational Activities, Inc., Freeport, L.I., NY 11520.

TEACHING AIDS

I. Childcraft offers a variety of materials to aid the child with letters, sounds, and words. These materials could also be used with games in Part III of text.

Tactile Letter Blocks. These large numbers and letters provide a kinesthetic experience which helps the child comprehend letter concepts. (Childcraft)

Touch Teaching Aids. These alphabet cards employ the tactile- kinesthetic method of instruction. The raised surface provides additional sensory experience which will speed recognition of letters for some children. (Childcraft)

Wonder Spelling Kit. This set contains 120 lower case and 26 capital letters in a natural finish plywood. (These could be used for many of the reading, spelling, and writing games in Part III.) (Childcraft)

These materials may be ordered from:

Childcraft Education Corporation
964 Third Ave.
New York, NY 10022

II. Educational Activities offers teaching materials to help the teacher with perceptual-motor activities.

Sound, Words, and Actions. This card file contains movement games to help build skills in language arts. The games fulfill the child's inherent need to move as well as helping to read and deal with words and letter symbols. (Educational Activities, Inc.)

A catalog of materials may be requested from:

Educational Activities, Inc.
Freeport, L.I., NY 11520

III. *Move-Grow-Learn* by Marianne Frostig is a movement education program to enhance the development of young children by improving physical, creative, and perceptual development. This program, designed for preschool and primary children, promotes good health, a sense of well-being and the development of sensory motor skills. It is also designed to develop self-awareness, awareness of time and space, and the ability to communicate, to interact with others, to perceive self in relation to environment, to solve problems, and to learn.

Follett Publishing Company
1018 West Washington Blvd.
Chicago, IL 60607

VIDEOTAPES

Data Based Gymnasium Training Tape, (Dunn & Moorehouse), with Jim Moorehouse. Oregon State University, Corvallis, OR 97331.

Project Unique Training Tape for "A Physical Fitness Test for the Physically Impaired." Joseph P. Winnick, State University of New York at Brockport, NY 11420.

Teaching Elementary Physical Education (Wessel): *Fundamental Motor Patterns*, VHS or ¾ U-matic; and *Class Management*, VHS or ¾ U-matic; Pro-Ed, 8700 Shoal Creek Blvd., Austin, TX 78758-6897.

HOMEMADE EQUIPMENT

Mats. Using a piece of 3' x 6' styrofoam 3" thick, cover it with a heavy piece of material (canvas, sail cloth) and sew it in place.

Jump ropes. A hank of sash cord or clothesline works nicely. The length of the rope should be approximately equal to the height of the child. The ends can be tied or taped to prevent unraveling.

Beanbags. Navy beans sewn in canvas or other suitable sturdy material is fine. Cut the material in 5" x 5" squares.

Beanbags of different shapes are also a good idea.

Balance beam. Make them about 8' in length using 2" x 4". If you construct this type of base, the beam can be either 2" or 4" in width.

Design A

Design B

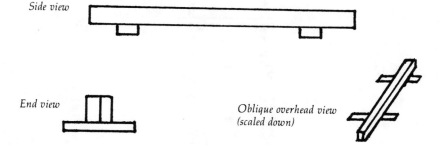

Side view

End view

Oblique overhead view
(scaled down)

Wands. Cut broom or mop handles into 3' to 4' sections. These wands or dowels can be used as lumni sticks, rhythm sticks, perceptual-motor wands for balance and gross motor skills, or exercise wands. In conjunction with other materials like crepe paper or rope they can be used as Chinese ribbon dance wands or rope ladders.

Balance board. Cut a piece of 3/4" plywood into a 15" square. Attach a small 2" x 2" block of wood in the middle of the square.

Painted patterns on available floor surface.

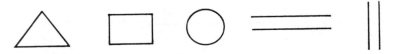

Footprints. Cut carpet squares work well.

Carpet Square

Rope ladders. With only three to seven drilled dowels, depending on preferences of length, ropes can be strung through and knotted to easily create an exciting and fitness-stimulating rope ladder. Hang these ladders from the wall, ceiling, or simply suspend them from another climbing apparatus to ensure a close, safe, and matted landing.

DEVELOPMENTAL MOTOR ACTIVITIES

Return lines. String-attached tee/wiffle balls and ping-pong balls are a help in eliminating the problems of ball retrieval, especially for the blind, aged, emotionally disturbed, or severely physically handicapped.

Ring-a-string ball jump. Use a rubber ring, or cut 19" of garden hose and tape to a circle. If the ends are joined to a small dowel, it is easier to form the ring. Then, tape a 2' to 3' string from the ring to a little ball. Insert the child's foot through the ring. Now instruct the child to get the ball circling round and round by jumping the ball and string on each pass with the other foot. Dance rhythms to music can evolve next.

Fine motor rope work. Simply balling up, tying, untying, braiding, and knotting rope helps increase fine motor strength, dexterity, and control.

Stilts. Of course, the old "rope and coffee can" stilts should not be forgotten. They do call for rather advanced skills in balance as well as total, sequential body-part integration.

Bounce boards. A plank set across two tires creates a very simple and effective bouncing board. The size of the tires, board, and child will dictate the possible elasticity of the activity.

Hoops. This is another piece of equipment of endless uses.

   a. *Hula hoops.* Black plastic plumbing tubing and plastic dowels are joined to form any size circle you desire. A standard size hoop is 8' in circumference and 1/2" thick. A 1 x 1/2" dowel is used to join the ends.

   b. *Skip trainers.* Children having difficulty learning how to skip often benefit by the use of hoops. They can be placed along the floor as shown with a specific color assigned to each foot. The child is instructed to set into the appropriate hoop, then take a hop with that same foot, then step into the next colored hoop with the other foot, and repeat. In a short time, the child will be able to increase the tempo, thereby resulting in a true skipping pattern: step, hop; step, hop; step, hop; step, hop.

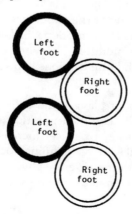

c. *Target practice.* Hoops with nets attached provide for retrieval of projectiles. They can be placed *behind* other smaller target orifices to aid in the retrieval process. Hoops standing vertically off the ground make great targets for balls, beanbags, or flying saucers.

d. *Obstacles.* Hoops can be set up alone or in long series to be used as obstacles through which to crawl, jump, dive, and swim.

Scooter boards. If caster wheels are available, homemade scooter boards become a reality. Make larger ones for children who need the area for balance (e.g., cerebral palsied, or myelodysplasias).

Slides and planes. Boards and planks can be set at inclined planes for scooter riding and climbing play. Inclined planes provide a great source of discovery with respect to which type of objects roll down it easily and which do not. Inclined planes an be carefully sanded and finished to make sliding boards. Also, with the application of a slippery surface like a shower curtain, the sliding board need not be sanded and finished so carefully.

Seesaws. With blocks for handles and the acquisition of a stable fulcrum, a seesaw can be realized.

Bowling ramps. Various-sized planks and boards make effective bowling ramps for the blind or severely physically handicapped. The ramp can be used in such games as modified horseshoes as well.

Adapted ping-pong. Boards mounted along the sides of a ping-pong table help keep the ball in play so that the game is not interrupted so often for ball retrieval.

Balls.

a. *Large therapy balls.* Large rubber or beach balls can be used very effectively in facilitating proper balance and equilibrium reactions while positioning the body in a way to inhibit inappropriate reactions. Relaxation and fun are additional by-products.

b. *Modifying organized sports and games.* The very young, very old, very frightened, and severely physically disabled (including quadriplegics) can enjoy and succeed in *beach ball* volleyball. The ball is slow, soft, safe, and easily tracked and returned even with a shrug of the shoulders, or a not of the head from those limited essentially to only these motions. *Balloons, tape and newspaper balls, and nerf balls* can also be used in modified volleyball as well as modified badminton, kickball, soccer, baseball. Long balloons allow for a slower moving but exciting football game.

Partially deflated soccer or playground balls provide a stimulating and safe adaptation to broomball. The incorporation of larger than usual balls into wheelchair/stretcher hockey or soccer increases the frequency of successful contacts and general ball control. Genuine hockey pucks in hockey or genuine soccer balls in soccer with the severely physically handicapped or mentally retarded would rarely be seen, let alone contacted or controlled.

Plastic bottles. These bottles are the epitome of versatility.

  a. *Scoops.* Plastic bottles can be cut in a way to make very effective implements for receipt and propulsion for balls, or beanbags for individual, partner, or group activities. In addition, these scoops can be used as shovels for sand, pebbles, or most anything.

  b. *Cones.* Plastic bottles can conveniently serve as obstacle course markers, goal markers, and end zone markers.

  c. *Weights.* The bottles can be filled with varying amounts of sand and used as exercise weights.

  d. *Arts and crafts.* The bottles can be painted or decorated into a variety of entertaining and useful animate or inanimate objects.

  e. *Target practice.* Plastic bottles may be easily utilized as safe and effective targets for rolling, throwing, kicking, and games (e.g., pitching practice, bowling, etc.).

  f. *Storage.* When the activities are finished, these bottles make great storage containers as they not only hold balls, bean bags, whatever, but they are self-stacking in that they also neatly hold each other.

Rhythm and Music. Instruments are limited in type and number only by the imagination.

  a. *Tambourines.* You can make these with pebbles or dried corn inside two aluminum pie pans. Another type of tambourine can be made by stringing a stiff wire through bottle caps into a circle. A third, fancier version can be fashioned from an embroidery hoop, muslin, and bottle caps nailed around the edges.

  b. *Drums.* Coffee cans, ice cream cartons, and similarly shaped containers provide the basic frame for building a drum.

  c. *Kazoos.* Don't forget to hum with a comb and paper—a loud, convenient, simple, cheap, and "never fail" horn.

Aquatics. Frequently, the use of various devices and toys during swimming instruction can serve to focus the child's attention away from being frightened by the water and onto the specific toy or task at hand. Children will often bob and dive for toys when they otherwise would refuse to get their face wet. Also, certain floatation devices serve therapeutic purposes in providing for optimal body position to facilitate relaxation and help inhibit inappropriate reactions.

  a. *Floatation devices.* This category includes vests, water wings, masks, goggles, snorkels, fins, lifesaving tubes, and belts. All can be utilized to stimulate relaxation and confidence in the individual and thereby to facilitate the optimal conditions for learning to take place.

  b. *Innertubes, rafts, and floatable toys.* Floatable toys often help children overcome their fear of the water when they see that their special toy does not sink away. Furthermore, many physically handicapped children have walked, hopped, jumped, and leaped for their first time ever when going after their special toy as it floats by them. The 80% reduction in the force of gravity allows for such achievements to take place, but the special toy is often the catalyst.

  c. *Sinkable toys.* Heavier toys are helpful aids in teaching children to emerge and descend. Toys that open and close like plastic Easter eggs can be opened and filled with water, allowing them to sink.

d. *Hoops.* Hoops are great for "musical bob under your hoop" games, underwater obstacle course swims, target practice, and relays.

e. *Kickboards.* Buy and cut some styrofoam appropriately. It is inexpensive and effective. The size, rigidity, and weight of kickboards make them effective baseball bats for blind children.

Safety helmet. Seizure-prone children who are integrated with nonseizure-prone children may be concerned about the attention brought to their headgear. Often, you can substitute bicycle, football, baseball batting, lacrosse, or wrestling headgear. The substitutes may provide even *more* protection in some cases. (If this isn't possible, you can compare their seizure headgear to the above types of helmets and headwear—the peer rejection may possibly transform into peer envy.)

Summary

Expensive equipment is rarely needed to implement an effective program of perceptual-motor learning. Instructors should not hesitate to manipulate the environment appropriately to achieve positive and meaningful experiences for all children, regardless of individual needs or exceptionalities. For example, the specialist should feel free to use larger, lighter, slower moving balls; lower baskets; more target sites; smaller target distances—whatever is necessary whenever indicated.

Homemade equipment can be used to stimulate and facilitate new areas of learning and success. The effectiveness of the equipment is dependent upon its appropriate incorporation with the specific population involved, the indicated program objectives, and the imagination and creativity of the individuals selecting and using it.

Appendix B: Sample Physician Referral Forms for Children With Exceptional Needs

Sample 1

CHILDREN'S MEDICAL CENTER
KLUGE CHILDREN'S REHABILITATION CENTER
DEPARTMENT OF RECREATIONAL THERAPY
ADAPTED PHYSICAL EDUCATION SECTION

UNIVERSITY OF VIRGINIA
HEALTH
SCIENCES
CENTER
CHILDREN'S MEDICAL CENTER

KLUGE CHILDREN'S REHABILITATION CENTER
AND RESEARCH INSTITUTE

ADAPTED PHYSICAL EDUCATION (APE) MEDICAL REFERRAL FORM

NAME: _____ DATE: _____

DIAGNOSIS: _____

_____

CONDITION

CONDITION IS: _____PERMANENT   _____TEMPORARY

COMMENTS:_____

_____

LENGTH OF RESTRICTION: _____

STUDENT REQUIRES USE OF: _____WHEELCHAIR _____CRUTCHES
_____OTHER _____

STUDENT SHOULD RETURN TO OUTPATIENT CLINIC FOR REEXAMINATION: ____

ACTIVITY RECOMMENDATIONS

INDICATE BODY AREAS IN WHICH MOVEMENT SHOULD BE ELIMINATED OR MINIMIZED.

	ELIMINATED	MINIMIZED	UNRESTRICTED	BOTH	LEFT	RIGHT
HEAD/NECK						
UPPER LIMBS						
LOWER LIMBS						
TRUNK						
OTHER						

SIGNED: _____ M.D.

APE SUGGESTIONS

THE FOLLOWING (REFER TO ATTACHMENT) ARE THERAPEUTIC AND PHYSICAL ACTIVITY
GUIDELINES RECOMMENDED FOR THIS STUDENT.

COMMENTS: _____

_____

_____

SIGNED: _____ STAFF THERAPIST DATE:_____

Courtesy: Ron Adams, Director of Therapeutic Recreation/Adapted Physical Education, Kluge Children's Rehabilitation Center and Research Institute, University of Virginia Medical Center, Charlottesville, VA 22901.

Sample 2

_____ Public Schools

_____ School

Physical Education Department

Special Physical Education Physician Referral/Permission Form

Student _____

Address _____

Phone # _____ Age _____ Date _____

   I hereby refer to you and give permission to you to include _____
student name
in your physical education program. I understand that your program provides special or adapted physical educational services for temporarily injured and permanently injured students.

   I am listing any types of exercises or activities that are *contraindicated* for this student here: _____

_____

_____

_____

_____

_____

_____

_____

_____

_____

(use back of page if needed)

Also, I am listing exercises or activities that are *particularly indicated or recommended,* for the student here: _____

_____

_____

_____

_____

_____

_____

_____

(use back of page if needed)

OTHER COMMENTS _____

_____

_____

_____

_____

_____

_____   _____

Physician's Signature   Date

_____

Physician's Name (please print)

Appendix C: Selected Organizations and Resources for Various Exceptionalities

For information concerning the sport of your choice, contact the respective organization or the PVA national sports coordinator at the National Office. Paralyzed Veterans of America, 801 Eighteenth Street, N.W., Washington, DC 20006.

ALL TERRAIN VEHICLES
Wheelchair Motorcycle Assoc., Inc.
101 Torrey Street
Brockton, MA 02401
(617) 583-8614

ARCHERY
National Wheelchair Athletic Assoc.
2107 Templeton Gap Road, Suite 3
Colorado Springs, CO 80907
(303) 632-0698

BASKETBALL
National Wheelchair Basketball Assoc.
110 Seaton Building
University of Kentucky
Lexington, KY 40506
(606) 257-1623

BOWLING
American Wheelchair Bowling Assoc.
Daryl Pfister
N54 W15858 Larkspur Lane
Menomonee Falls, WI 53051

BOWLING AIDS
George Snyder
5809 N.E. 21st Avenue
Fort Lauderdale, FL 33308

Recreation Unlimited
820 Woodend Road
Stratford, CT 06497
(203) 384-0802

CEREBRAL PALSY
National Assoc. of Sports for Cerebral
    Palsy
66 East 34th Street
New York, NY 10016
(212) 481-6345

HORSEBACK RIDING
North American Riding for the Handi-
    capped Association
Box 100
Ashburn, VA 22011
(703) 471-1621

NATIONAL PARK GUIDE ACCESS
National Parks
Superintendent of Documents
Washington, DC 20402
(202) 783-3238 (price $3.50)

SKIING
Colorado Outdoor Education Center
P.O. Box 697
Breckenridge, CO 80424
(303) 453-6422

Winter Park Handicap Program
P.O. Box 313
Winter Park, CO 80482
(303) 726-5514

National Handicapped Sports and
    Recreation Association
P.O. Box 18664
Capitol Hill Station
Denver, CO 80218

SKIING EQUIPMENT ARROYA
Beneficial Designs
5858 Empire Grade
Santa Cruz, CA 95060
(408) 429-8447

Smith Sled
Mountainsmith, Inc.
12790 West 6th Place
Golden, CO 80401
(303) 238-5823

Sit & Ski
Mountainman Industries
720 Front Street
Bozeman, MT 59715
(406) 587-0310

SOFTBALL
National Wheelchair Softball Assoc.
P.O. Box 737
Sioux Falls, SD 57101

SWIMMING
National Wheelchair Athletic Assoc.
(See Archery)

TABLE TENNIS
National Wheelchair Athletic Assoc.
(See Archery)

TENNIS
National Foundation of Wheelchair
    Tennis
3857 Birch Street, #411
Newport Beach, CA 92660

Peter Burwash International
2203 Timberloch Place, Suite 126
The Woodlands, TX 77380
(713) 363-4707

TRACK AND FIELD
National Wheelchair Athletic Assoc.
(See Archery)

WEIGHTLIFTING
National Wheelchair Athletic Assoc.
(See Archery)

WHEELCHAIR SPORTS MAGAZINE
Sports 'n Spokes
5201 North 19th Avenue, Suite 111
Phoenix, AZ 85015
(602) 246-9426

WILDERNESS RECREATION
Minnesota Outward Bound School
Box 250
Long Lake, MN 55356
(612) 473-5476

Vinland Center
3675 Induhapi Road
Loretto, MN 55357
(612) 479-3555

NATIONAL HANDICAPPED SPORTS CHAPTERS AND AFFILIATES

ALASKA

Challenge Alaska
ATTN: Patrick Reinhart
P.O. Box 110065
Anchorage, AK 99511-0065
(907) 563-2658

Access Alaska
ATTN: Rick Tessadore
3550 Airport Way, Suite 3
Fairbanks, AK 99709
(907) 479-7940

CALIFORNIA

NHSRA of Southern California
The Unrecables
ATTN: Linda Fryback
2210 Glick Court
Redondo Beach, CA 90278
(213) 374-6775

San Diego Adventures
ATTN: Kent Bry
1105 First Street
Encinitas, CA 92024
(619) 942-2188

NHSRA of Orange County
ATTN: Bon & Janet Beutner
531 Heather Ave.
La Habra, CA 90631
(213) 697-0351

NHSRA, Northern California Chapter
ATTN: Douglas J. Pringle
5926 Illinois Ave.
Orangevale, CA 90631
(916) 989-0402

Cal STAR
Dept. of Recreational Sports
University of California
ATTN: Ann Fitzgerald
2301 Bancroft Way
Berkeley, CA 94720
(415) 642-8342

NHSRA of Fresno
ATTN: Virginia Gryalva
P.O. Box 15263
Fresno, CA 93702
(209) 252-6126

Mother Lode Chapter
ATTN: Richard K. Van Aken
P.O. Box 4274
Camp Connell, CA 95223
(209) 795-5288

COLORADO

Breckenridge Outdoor Education
    Center For The Handicapped
P.O. Box 697
Breckenridge, CO 80424
(303) 453-6422

Crested Butte Physically
    Challenged Skier Program
ATTN: Robin Norton
P.O. Box A
Mount Crested Butte, CO 81225
(303) 349-2333

Durango/Purgatory Handicapped Sports
    Association
ATTN: Lisa Margol
P.O. Box 8333
Durango, CO 81301
(303) 247-9000

Rocky Mountain Handicapped
    Sportsmen's Association
ATTN: Tom Reetz
1315 S. Eaton Ct.
Lakewood, CO 80226
(303) 934-9540

Winter Park Sports and Learning
    Center
ATTN: Paul Di Bello
P.O. Box 36
Winter Park, CO 80482
(303) 892-0961

Aspen Handicapped Skiers Assoc.
ATTN: Edwin H. Lucks
P.O. Box 5429
Snowmass Village, CO 81615
(303) 923-3294

Colorado Discovery Ability
ATTN: April Black
P.O. Box 400
Mesa, CO 81643
(303) 268-5573

Challenge West
ATTN: Rick L. Maez
1101 E. Columbia
Colorado Springs, CO 80903
(719) 630-8329

CONNECTICUT

Connecticut Handicapped Ski
    Foundation
ATTN: Sal Ucello
599 Graham Road
South Windsor, CT 06074
(203) 644-1322

D.C., MARYLAND, VIRGINIA

Nation's Capital Chapter
ATTN: Frank Stowell/Kathy Harbert
4937 West Chalk Point Road
West River, MD 20778
(301) 571-0217/868-9280/
261-5075

FLORIDA

NHSRA, South Florida Chapter
ATTN: George DePontis
P.O. Box 370788
Miami, FL 33137
(305) 751-2525

GEORGIA

NHSRA, Atlanta Chapter
ATTN: Sean Shipley
P.O. Box 327
Clarkston, GA 30021
(404) 498-7204

IDAHO

Association for Handicapped Recreation
    Inc.
ATTN: Executive Director
P.O. Box 2451
Coer d'Alene, ID 83814

Recreation Unlimited, Inc.
ATTN: Caroline Vogel
P.O. Box 447
Boise, ID 83702
(208) 383-6595

ILLINOIS

Chicagoland Handicapped Skiers
ATTN: Valerie Byrne
1086 Briarcliffe
Wheaton, IL 60187
(312) 682-4018

INDIANA

Greater Indianapolis Chapter
Handicapped Skiing
ATTN: Tony Williams
c/o Indianapolis Parks & Recreation
    Department
1426 West 29th Street
Indianapolis, IN 46208
(317) 634-0988

Calumet Region Chapter
ATTN: Jackson Ivery II
5032 Kennedy Ave.
East Chicago, IN 46312
(219) 391-9099

Special Outdoor Leisure Opportunities,
    Inc.
ATTN: Marilyn Calahan
P.O. Box 6221
South Bend, IN 46660

IOWA

Sundown Handicapped Skiers
ATTN: Thomas W. Gavin
Sundown Ski Area
9000 Asbury Road
Dubuque, IA 52001
(319) 556-6676

MASSACHUSSETTS, MAINE

Wachusett Mountain Education
    Foundation
ATTN: Kathy Chandler
499 Mountain Road
Princeton, MA 01541
(508) 464-5101

New England Handicapped Sportsmen's
    Association
ATTN: Earl Plummer
26 McFarlin Road
Chelmsford, MA 01824
(508) 256-3240

MICHIGAN

Michigan Handicapped Sports and
    Recreation Association
ATTN: Lee Helms
238 Woodview Court, Apt. 244
Rochester Hills, MI 48063-6041
(313) 853-0648

Cannonsburg Challenged Skiers
    Association
ATTN: Theresa Rettig
1722 Widdicomb, N.W.
Grand Rapids, MI 49504
(616) 531-2391

MINNESOTA

Courage Alpine Skiers
ATTN: Neal Manecke
3523 Arbor Lane
Minnetonka, MN 55343
(612) 938-1724

Twin Ports Flyers
ATTN: Mary Lou Donovan
Courage Center
205 W. 2nd St. #451
Duluth, MN 55802
(218) 727-6874

MONTANA

I Am Third Foundation
dba Eagle Mount
ATTN: Kathy Wells
P.O. Box 3118
Bozeman, MT 59772
(406) 586-1781

Dream-Big Mountain Disabled Ski
    Program
ATTN: Dennis Jones
P.O. Box 1058
Kalispell, MT 59903
(406) 862-3511

NEVADA

Northern Nevada Ski School for the
    Disabled
ATTN: Rosemary Dixon
P.O. Box 6244
Incline Village, NV 89450
(702) 832-0480

Lakeside Chapter
City of Las Vegas
ATTN: Roy Post
749 Veterans Memorial Drive
Las Vegas, NV 89101
(702) 648-2377

NEW HAMPSHIRE

Northeast Passage Outing Club
ATTN: Jill Gravink
Northeast Rehabilitation Hospital
70 Butler Street
Salem, NH 03079
(603) 893-2900 ext. 472

NEW MEXICO

Lovelace/Sandia Peak Ski Program
ATTN: Pat McGowan
2425 Ridgecrest Drive SE
Albuquerque, NM 87108
(505) 766-4755

NEW YORK

NHSRA of New York
ATTN: Dan Weirman
508 Verna Drive
Endwell, NY 13760
(607) 758-6960

Disabled Ski Program at Ski Windham
ATTN: Gwen C.B. Allard
EPSIA Educational Foundation
1-A Lincoln Ave.
Albany, NY 12205-4900
(518) 452-6095

NORTH CAROLINA

YMCA Wake County, Inc.
ATTN: Candice Matthews
1012 Oberlin Road
Raleigh, NC 27065
(919) 828-3205

OHIO

Three Trackers of Ohio
ATTN: Joan Seitz
562 Elko Ave.
Akron, OH 44305
(216) 733-1525

OREGON

Flying Outriggers Ski Club
ATTN: Jolene M. Corey
211 Oregon Pioneer Building
Portland, OR 97204-2672
(503) 222-1327

Mount Hood Handicap Ski Association,
Inc.
ATTN: Ralph Summers
P.O. Box 15071
Portland, OR 97217
(503) 230-6108

Shared Outdoor Adventure Recreation
P.O. Box 14583
ATTN: Dave Espeseth
Portland, OR 98214
(503) 283-1613

PENNSYLVANIA

Three Rivers Adaptive Sports
c/o Harmarsville Rehabilitation Center
ATTN: Harry Scaggs
P.O. Box 11460, Guys Run Road
Pittsburgh, PA 15238
(412) 535-1389

The Philadelphia Area Handicapped
Skiing Club
ATTN: Isabel Bohn/Ned Goodrich
P.O. Box 884, 28 Simpson Road
Ardmore, PA 19003
(215) 848-3666

Good Shepherd Rehabilitation Hospital
ATTN: Sarah Boyer, CTRA
T.R. Dept.
5th and St. John Streets
Allentown, PA 18103

Deutsch Institute Applied Research
Center
ATTN: Deborah Moran
403 Chamber of Commerce Building
Mulberry and Washington Ave.
Scranton, PA 18503
(717) 348-1968

SOUTH CAROLINA

Palmetto Players
ATTN: Linda Lake
212 Netherland Drive
Irmo, SC 29063
(803) 781-6834

TEXAS

Southwest Wheelchair Athletic
Association
ATTN: Judy Einbinder
1475 West Gray, Suite 161
Houston, TX 77019
(713) 522-9769

UTAH

Paul Hill Adaptive Sports Association
ATTN: Quintin Gray
98 Roosevelt Ave.
American Forks, UT 84003
(801) 756-5537

Park City Handicapped Sports
   Association
ATTN: Meeche White
P.O. Box 680286
Park City, UT 84068
(801) 649-3991

Utah Handicapped Skiers Association
ATTN: Steve Peterson
P.O. Box 108
Roy, UT 84067
(801) 777-4515

VERMONT

Vermont Handicapped Ski Foundation
ATTN: Laura C. Perry
P.O. Box 261, Rt. 44
Brownsville, VT 05037
(802) 484-7711 ext. 3005

VIRGINIA

Woodrow Wilson Rehabilitation Center
ATTN: Diane Huss
Fisherville, VA 22939
(703) 332-7000

WASHINGTON

Seattle Handicapped Sports &
   Recreation Association
ATTN: Sheri Baylin
P.O. Box 75614
Seattle, WA 98125
(206) 363-6510

WEST VIRGINIA

The Challenge Athletes of Silver Creek,
   West Virginia
ATTN: Gary Morriston
P.O. Box 150
Slatyfork, WV 26291
(304) 572-4000

Index